OTHER BOOKS BY STANLEY TURKEL

- Heroes of the American Reconstruction (2005)
- Great American Hoteliers: Pioneers of the Hotel Industry (2009)
- Built To Last: 100+ Year-Old Hotels in New York (2011)
- Built To Last: 100+ Year-Old Hotels East of the Mississippi (2013)
- Hotel Mavens: Lucius M. Boomer, George C. Boldt and Oscar of the Waldorf (2014)
- Great American Hoteliers Volume 2: Pioneers of the Hotel Industry (2016)
- Built To Last: 100+ Year-Old Hotels West of the Mississippi (2017)

HOTEL MAVENS

Volume 2

Henry Morrison Flagler, Henry Bradley Plant, Carl Graham Fisher

STANLEY TURKEL, CMHS

authorHOUSE®

AuthorHouse™
1663 Liberty Drive
Bloomington, IN 47403
www.authorhouse.com
Phone: 1 (800) 839-8640

Published by AuthorHouse   07/18/2018

ISBN: 978-1-5462-3985-7 (sc)
ISBN: 978-1-5462-3983-3 (hc)
ISBN: 978-1-5462-3984-0 (e)

Library of Congress Control Number: 2018907074

Print information available on the last page.

Any people depicted in stock imagery provided by Getty Images are models, and such images are being used for illustrative purposes only.
Certain stock imagery © Getty Images.

This book is printed on acid-free paper.

CONTENTS

DEDICATION

To my amazing children and their mates:

- Marc Turkel and Meredith Dinneen
- Allison Turkel and Toni Robinson
- Joshua and Susan Forrest
- Benay Forrest

FOREWORD

By Sean Hennessey, President, Lodging Advisors

In this book, Stanley Turkel tells the fascinating stories of three "hotel mavens" who made Florida into one of the world's most famous tourist destinations. Henry Morrison Flagler, Henry Bradley Plant and Carl Graham Fisher are true legends whose business acumen and zeal for development led them to the same fertile ground: Florida in the 1920s. The land boom occurring in Florida at that time was so famous that it was the theme of the Marx Brothers movie "The Cocoanuts", with Groucho Marx as the proprietor of the Hotel de Cocoanut. To our good fortune, Flagler, Plant and Fischer had significantly better luck than did Groucho.

These three mavens exhibited visionary ambition that broke with tradition and shifted the direction of the hospitality industry. Prior to the 1920s, travel was primarily for business purposes and available accommodations were primarily utilitarian. But with the development of spectacular resorts by these mavens, Americans developed an aspirational desire to vacation in luxurious style. The resorts built by these men changed travelers expectations from merely visiting a new area to being swept into a fantasy world of luxury accommodations, haute cuisine, and exceptional service. Hotel stays changed from having the comforts of home to an experience which could never be gotten at home. This ideal continues to this day, as the best hotels strive to surprise and delight their guests.

The appeal of the Sunshine State's tropical climate, lush landscape, and sand beaches has only grown over the years: it is now the 3rd most populous state in the country and the 8th most densely populated. Florida is not immune to the ill effects of economic downturns but it has always come roaring back to popularity and growth. It seems that the state has captured the imaginations of all who have visited: from Ponce de Leon- who has created a vast entertainment empire built upon an image Jimmy Buffet – who has created a vast entertainment empire built upon an image of Florida as a carefree wonderland.

The lessons that can be drawn from these stored hoteliers should resonate with students of the business today. For example, Henry Flagler thoughtfully provided for his employees welfare as a fundamental attribute of successful operations; is there any more pressing issue in the hotel industry today than developing excellent staff? All three mavens knew that the resorts needed an excellent transportation infrastructure to thrive. All three also knew that the resorts don't exist in isolation but require an attractive, thriving local community to enhance the guest experience and make success sustainable. Stanley's telling of these men's stories brings out these important truths much more vividly than any academic text on the hotel of the business.

Although this book is about these three hotel mavens, I would be remiss not to mention a maven of hotel history, our author Stanley Turkel. Stanley merits this accolade just as surely as the men who created the great Florida resorts. Prior to Stanley's efforts, the history of famous hotels and great hoteliers was given limited treatment in scattered sources. Stanley has been zealously researching and telling the stories behind famous hot1els and hoteliers for many years now, and his books provide a compendium of the people and places that have left their mark on the hotel industry. His writing is crisp and his stories are compelling. I hope he continues to mine this rich vein for years to come.

It's often said that the hotels are a "people business", meaning that guests have the best stay when the hotel employees truly care about each guest. The best way to capture the essence of this "people business", then, is to understand those hoteliers who excelled at touching people's lives. And there is no better way to learn about these leaders than through Stanley Turkel's books. It's hard to overstate how important his tireless efforts in telling these stories are for the hotel industry and its leaders. Just as Flagler, Plant and Fisher created resorts that will stand for ages, Stanley's histories will endure, educate, and delight readers for ages to come.

Sean Hennessey is an Assistant Professor at the Jonathan M. Tisch Center for Hospitality and Tourism at NYU's School of Professional Studies. He is also the President of Lodging Advisors, a firm that advises hotel investors.

PREFACE

My long-time preoccupation with hotel history reveals one continuous strand: the achievements of unique entrepreneurs who created singular hotels one at a time. These pioneers were not by subsequent definition, "hotel men". They did not attend hotel schools because there were none until 1924 with the creation of the Cornell School of Hotel Administration. Most of them did not grow up in the hotel business but became successful because of their varied on-the-job training experiences, business acumen and unexpected opportunities. Their tradition-breaking vision and single-minded ambition led them to create iconic hotels. My research has uncovered three such hotel mavens two of whom 1) were both essentially in the railroad and steamship business 2) were friendly competitors 3) concentrated their hotel creations in the state of Florida: Henry Morrison Flagler on the east coast and Henry Bradley Plant on the west coast. The third genius was Carl Graham Fisher who created Miami Beach.

Because they built, acquired, renovated and operated hotels, they all three qualify as "hotel mavens". The word "maven is defined by the following:

- Wikipedia:
    "trusted expert in a particular field who seeks to pass knowledge on to others"

- The New Thesaurus:
    "someone who is dazzlingly skilled in any field; hotshot, superstar, virtuoso, wizard, sensation, star, ace, genius, champion"
- Synonyms:
    Ace, artist, authority, cognoscente, connoisseur, crackerjack, guru, maestro, master, expert, scholar, shark, virtuoso, whiz, Renaissance man.

The word "maven" comes from the Yiddish language and means one who understands life based on an accumulation of knowledge. It was first recorded (spelled mayvin) in English in 1950 (in the *Jewish Standard* of Toronto) and popularized in the United States in the 1960s. It was used in a series of commercials created by Martin Solow for Vita Herring Company featuring "The Beloved Herring Maven" which ran in radio ads from 1964 to 1968 and then brought back in 1983. An example of one such print advertisement:

> "Get Vita at your favorite supermarket, grocery or delicatessen. Tell them the beloved Maven sent you. It won't save you any money but you'll get the best herring".

In the 1980s, the word became more common when the *New York Times* columnist William Safire adapted it to describe himself as "the language maven."

The popular author Malcolm Gladwell used the term in his book *The Tipping Point* (Little Brown, 2000) to describe those who are intense gatherers of information and impressions, and are often the first to pick up on new or nascent trends. Gladwell also suggested that mavens may act most effectively when in collaboration with connectors – i.e., those people who have wide network of casual acquaintances by whom they are trusted, often a network that crosses many social boundaries and groups.

In my estimate, the term hotel maven is most appropriate to describe Flagler, Plant and Fisher who could be described as the most creative men of their time. They each developed multiple hotels: Flagler to enhance his Florida East Coast Railroad route and Plant on the west coast of Florida to enhance his Southern Express Railway Company and Fisher to develop the city of Miami Beach and the Montauk area on Long Island, N.Y.

ACKNOWLEDGMENTS

I wrote my first book, "Heroes of the American Reconstruction: Profiles of Sixteen Educators, Politicians and Activists" in 2005. It was published by McFarland & Company, Inc. Jefferson, North Carolina. It took me nine years to research and write it.

This book, "Hotel Mavens Volume Two: Henry Morrison Flagler, Henry Bradley Plant and Carl Graham Fisher" took one year to research and write. The difference reflects my indebtedness to the new digital world and the computer technology that has revolutionized historical research. For most of my adult life, it was necessary to visit the libraries that housed the books needed for research, search the index files, find the books you needed, and wait in the library reading rooms until the librarians searched the stacks, found those books and delivered them to your desk. Then you researched those books for the information that you needed to write your thesis. My earliest efforts required me to copy the information longhand because copying machines had not yet been invented.

The internet and Google has changed all that. Now the computer on my desk in my home office has become the portal to websites that provide access to most of the book collections, manuscript archives, newspaper articles and a huge variety of pertinent publications.

The availability of digitalized files made ready accessibility easier than I could have imagined. Nevertheless, it still requires an author to have a singular idea to explore and research. In order for the book to be successful, it must examine the idea with vigor and present a thesis that tells an interesting story in a readable style.

The triumvirate of Henry Morrison Flagler, Henry Bradley Plant and Carl Graham Fisher created Florida as we know it today. While none of them planned the complete vacation paradise, they each started with the creation of transportation: Flagler and Plant with railroads; Fisher with bicycles and automobiles. For a miraculous period of extraordinary accomplishments, they transformed the state of Florida with spectacular hotels. Their stories are worth researching and reporting.

Henry Morrison Flagler (1830-1913):

Several figures stand out in the development of Florida into a world-class tourist destination, including Walt Disney and his predecessors, Addison Mizner, Carl Graham Fisher and Henry Bradley Plant. The earliest and arguably the most influential of Florida's early developers, however, was Henry Morrison Flagler, who invented the concept of the Florida vacation as we know it today. He ultimately extended the Florida East Coast Railway the length of Florida's 1,197 mile coastline.

Henry Morrison Flagler left his home in western New York in 1844 at 14 years of age to join his half-brother, Daniel M. Harkness, in Republic, Ohio. The frugal home Henry was leaving had been occupied by many Flaglers before him. His American lineage traced back to Zacharra Flegler (as the name was then spelled) who, with his wife, two small sons and a baby daughter, left England for America in January 1710. With the other family members, they settled in Columbia and Ulster counties in upstate New York. Flegler married a third time after his first two wives died prematurely. All of the American Flaglers are descended from one or the other of the three sons of Zacharra Flegler – Philip, Simon and Zachariah.

To Zacharia Flegler and his three wives were born 16 children, most of whom grew up and settled in Dutchess County. Solomon

Flegler, the eighth child, was born on May 8, 1760 and subsequently became the grandfather of Henry Morrison Flagler. Solomon made at least one major contribution to the family. He changed the spelling from Flegler to Flagler. Solomon and his wife, Ester, had 11 children. Their fifth child, Isaac Flagler, was born on April 22, 1787 and he became the father of Henry Morrison Flagler.

Henry's mother, Elizabeth Flagler, had been married twice before. Her first husband was Hugh Morrison of Washington County, New York. Her second husband was David Harkness, a physician of Bellevue, Ohio who died in 1825. The large and prominent Harkness family would later provide career opportunities for Henry Flagler. Elizabeth married Isaac Flagler with a ready-made family, consisting of young Dan Harkness and Carrie Flagler. On January 2, 1830, Henry Morrison Flagler was born when Dan was eight and Carrie was five. Despite the eight year difference in their ages, Henry and his half brother Daniel Harkness got along very well. At age 15, Daniel left home for Bellevue where he got a job as a salesman in the store of L.G. Harkness and Company.

A few years later, young Henry, tall and handsome for his age, was eager to leave farm life in Medina, New York to seek his own fortune. His father, Isaac Flagler, was a poor preacher-farmer who had served several Presbyterian congregations in Western New York and northern Ohio. Henry worked on a small boat headed for Buffalo in exchange for his fare. Early on the second day away from home, Henry found another boat headed for Sandusky, Ohio. The trip across Lake Erie was rough and lasted three days and nights. Henry was seasick and unhappy until the boat reached Sandusky. Nevertheless, on the very next day, young Henry went to work for L.G. Harkness and Company under the watchful eye of Dan Harkness, whose uncle Lamont Harkness owned a general store business.

Henry's on-the-job business education expanded during his three-year employment at the general store in Republic. Besides salesmanship, he learned the lifelong good habits of thrift, ingenuity and good judgment. While working under Dan and Lamon Harkness's supervision, he acquired a sense of commercial values and learned the rudiments of a profitable business. When Dan was promoted and became a member of a new firm named Chapman, Harkness and Company, Henry took Dan's place as manager of the store in Republic. After five years, Henry was promoted to a job with Chapman, Harkness and Company where his salary was increased to nearly $400 a year. In Bellevue, Ohio Henry met and married Mary Harkness on November 9, 1853 when he was twenty-three years old.

While Dan Harkness and Henry Flagler were in business in shipping grain and making liquor, Stephen V. Flagler cooperated to their mutual benefit. Flagler spent much time with Stephen learning about the distillery business. In addition to wines and liquors, Stephen dealt in grain, livestock, and banking. He was accustomed to big money deals and always traded on a larger scale than did the two other liquor makers in Bellevue. After several years in the business, Flagler sold out, but not before making a sizeable fortune. Dan Harkness, who took over Flagler's liquor interest, did not sell the Bellevue distillery, which was part of Harkness and Company, until 1868.

Stephen Harkness's big money haul in the distillery business came with the first comprehensive Internal Revenue Act of July 1, 1862. Among other things, the law included a tax upon malt and distilled liquors. Prior to the passing of the law, Senator John Sherman, sponsor of the Sherman Anti-Trust Act, warned Harkness of its significance. Sherman, who was on the United States Senate Finance Committee, had inside information. He foresaw a tax of $2 on each gallon of spirits. Harkness immediately set forth to accumulate an abundant stock before the law went into effect. He used all his reserve to buy up supplies of whiskey so that he could sell it at the higher price when the tax was enacted.

The local bank in Monroeville, which he owned, felt the strain of Harkness's determination to buy up all the whiskey he could find. Farmers who had funds on deposit became alarmed when they heard of the Harkness scheme, especially those who had difficulty cashing their corn receipts. Harkness employed Hiram Latham to assure the anxious farmers that "old Steve Harkness" was all right, and that his intentions were sound and good. But Latham did not get very far in trying to persuade the farmers that Harkness was not building his own fortune at their expense.

Harkness criticized John D. Rockefeller, who acted as commission merchant for him as well as for his acquaintances in Bellevue. It seems that when Rockefeller delayed payment for a shipment of grain, Harkness sent the following message: "Why…. don't you remit for the last car of corn I shipped you? Unless I get it soon I will bust." Harkness's business was stocked from cellar to ceiling with all sorts of whiskey and wines. He sold out his stock at the advanced price without having to pay the tax and made over $300,000 clear profit. In 1866, he sold his property in Monroeville and moved to Cleveland, where he continued to invest in various business interests for a number of years.

Mary and Henry Flagler lived in Bellevue from 1853 until 1862 among their friends and relatives and became a part of an expanding community. During this time, the argument between the North and the South over slavery was rapidly reaching a breaking point. Flagler, a keen student of national affairs, watched with much interest the situation in Kansas following the passage of the Kansas-Nebraska Act in 1854 and the decision in the Dred Scott case in 1857 which held that "a negro, whose ancestors were imported (into the U.S.), and sold as slaves… could not be an American citizen…." Flagler was aware of the significance of the Republican victory in 1860, and was not surprised when the Southern states began to secede from the Union and started the Civil War.

Flagler shared the views of most fellow Ohioans on slavery and strongly favored a compromise with the South. When Lincoln issued his call for volunteers in 1861, Dan Harkness was one of the first to offer his services to the Union Army, but Flagler did not do so. John D. Rockefeller, Philip Armour and John Wanamaker also did not enlist. During the Civil War, men aged 18 to 45 had several options provided by federal law to avoid conscription: pay a substitute to take your place or pay a commutation fee of $300 enabling you to avoid service.

The Civil War increased the volume of Flagler's grain business. He routed grain purchased by the United States government to the federal troops, a transaction which meant great financial returns for him. While his fortune was growing in Bellevue, his family, to which he gave much attention, was also increasing. He was fond of children, and was pleased when his first child, Jennie Louise, arrived on March 18, 1855. A second child was born on June 18, 1858, and was named Carrie for his half sister. Sadly, little

Carrie was never well and died when she was only three years old. Their youngest child, Harry Harkness Flagler, was born a number of years later. Mary was never robust and many of the home responsibilities were undertaken by Henry. From childhood, Mary's health had to be safeguarded. They usually spent their evenings at home and very seldom did either seek entertainment in other places.

Both Mary and Henry were religious and participated as frequently as her health would permit in all activities of the Presbyterian church. Their closest associates were Isabella and Dan Harkness; Isabella had always been Mary's favorite sister and the relations between Dan and Henry were warm. In fact, the four seemed like one family since Isabella and Mary were sisters, Dan and Henry were half brothers, and Isabella and Dan were first cousins. Mary's parents were frequent visitors at the Flagler's modest home. In 1855, Henry's parents retired and moved to Bellevue to spend their last years. With them came Carrie Flagler, the half-sister who had always been a favorite. L. G. Harkness prided himself upon his three sons-in-law, Dan Harkness, Henry Flagler, and Barney York. The three young men remained fast friends all of their lives. Isabella and Dan Harkness had five children; all but one, however, died in early infancy. When Dan went into the Union Army in 1861, he left a despondent wife who never fully recovered from the loss of her babies. Mary and Henry Flagler lost their second child during their residence in Bellevue and Mary had one or two serious illnesses which kept her husband worried for a long time. Henry's mother died in 1861 and his father's health was poor until his death a number of years later.

Flagler's father-in-law, L. G. Harkness, was the first person from Bellevue to be attracted by the abundant deposits of salt discovered around Saginaw, Michigan. He already had extensive interests in the lumber business in Michigan. As soon as the boom began, he realized the possibility in producing salt and brought a large block of shares in the East Saginaw Salt Manufacturing Company. For the first two years, Harkness was pleased with the profits he made from the venture. It was at this time, in 1862, that Henry M. Flagler yielded to the temptation of casting his fortune in this new and uncertain industry. He pulled up stakes in Bellevue and moved his family to Saginaw in the hope of becoming a wealthy man in record time. Flagler sank his savings of $50,000 into a new firm named the Flagler and York Salt Company. Many other speculators had the same idea and several new salt-producing companies were formed in Saginaw in 1862 and 1863.

From the start, Flagler liked Saginaw, and was happy to be part of so progressive a community. Although Mary Flagler continued to be in poor health, the presence of her sister, Julia York, kept her from becoming despondent among so many strangers. The Flaglers took an active interest in the community, especially in religious activities. The Flaglers affiliated with the Congregational Church. Before many months had passed, Flagler was made superintendent of the Sunday School, a position for which he was well qualified. Until his departure from Saginaw in 1865, he continued his work, not only in the Sunday School, but also as a member of the Board of Trustees of the Church.

For about two years, Flagler made money in the salt business but the many processes of manufacture were never completely mastered by the get-rich-quick investors. Flagler soon learned this fact and the one thing which drove Flagler out of salt production was the keen competition in Michigan and Ohio which cut down drastically on profits. Because of the collapse of salt prices at the close of the Civil War, Flagler not only lost the $50,000 that he had sunk in the venture, but, in addition, was $50,000 in debt. The loss made him cautious about speculating on anything until he had had thoroughly investigated its merits and possibilities. The nation was crippled and bruised from four years of the bloodiest war in history with 750,000 dead out of a population of only 30 million. The passage of the 13th, 14th and 15th amendments to the Constitution was called the second Bill of Rights and helped to stimulate the post-war Reconstruction period.

Henry Flagler was 35 years-old when the Civil War ended. He chose Cleveland as the place where he would try to remake his fortune because in 1865, it was one of the leading towns in Ohio with about 45,000 people and was strategically located. When Flagler arrived, the city had transportation facilities that were almost unrivaled. Situated on Lake Erie, it had access to the other Great Lakes and the Erie Canal. It was served by five railroads: the Cleveland, Columbus and Cincinnati; the Cleveland and Pittsburgh; the Lake Shore Railroad, which connected with the Erie and the New York Central; the Cleveland and Toledo; and the Cleveland and Mahoning; the Atlantic and Great Western was added a few years later. In 1860, there were no more than 30,600 miles of railroad in the United States, but that was great progress over the 2,818 miles in 1840. Flagler's family accompanied him to Cleveland, refusing to remain in Bellevue until he was settled. They rented a modest home and with only a few hundred dollars, which his father-in-law forwarded to him, Flagler set himself up in the grain business. Since he had made money in it before, he had hopes of doing so again. It was a slow start for Flagler, who was impatient and anxious to begin to pay back his debts. On the side, he became associated with a concern which made barrels, a venture that proved a failure. In another effort to make money quickly, he tried to market a specially-built horseshoe which was his own creation, but this scheme also fell through. For the first time in his career, Henry Flagler was discouraged and about ready to quit. Everything seemed to be against him. Bellevue, with all that the Harknesses had to offer there, seemed more inviting than ever before. He remarked to a friend one day that if he ever paid off his debts and was $10,000 ahead, he would retire from business. Fortunately, this loss of enthusiasm and desire to make a fortune did not last long.

In 1866, Maurice B. Clark, a grain commission merchant, offered Flagler a job with his firm, Clark and Sanford. Maurice Clark was a young Englishman who was about the same age as Flagler. Before the formation of Clark and Sanford, he had been associated with Otis, Brownell and Company, probably the oldest grain dealer in Cleveland. For a while, he was associated with John D. Rockefeller in the same kind of business and it was then that Clark and Rockefeller became acquainted with Flagler. In 1865, the Clark and Rockefeller partnership dissolved. Rockefeller followed his oil interests while Clark remained in the grain business and looked for an experienced new partner. Flagler took the job Clark offered, but did not invest any money in the partnership. He enjoyed his association with Clark and ably filled the place left by Rockefeller. This marked a turning point in Henry Flagler's life. Clark gave him considerable authority in the business. He had freedom to act as if he were an investor and a partner. Flagler met with success from the start and within a few months the firm began to show a noticeable increase in its volume of business. Flagler's commissions increased each month and he began to think in terms of large sums again. By 1867, he owed less than $30,000 on the $50,000 he had borrowed from the Harknesses.

The Flaglers moved into a larger home on Euclid Avenue. There were nine rooms in their two-story house, some of which were often occupied by relatives. In 1870, his father-in-law, L. G. Harkness, came to live with them after retiring from his business in Bellevue. In that same year, Mary Flagler gave birth to their third child, a son, Harry Harkness Flagler.

Flagler's friends were influential and some of them were exceedingly wealthy. Stephen V. Harkness, who moved to Cleveland in 1866 after selling his liquor business in Monroeville, was an intimate associate. His fortune, one of the largest in the city, continued to increase through his efforts in real estate. Mary Flagler, Stephen's first cousin, was his favorite relative. As her physical infirmities grew worse with the years, Stephen shared Henry's growing concern over her condition. He was a regular visitor in the Flagler home and enjoyed their hospitality on many a winter evening.

Flagler's business again brought him into contact with John D. Rockefeller, whom he had known since the days he had worked as a grain dealer in Bellevue. Their acquaintance grew into a friendship. The early years of the two men were quite different. Rockefeller, born in Richford, New York on July 8, 1839, was nine years younger than Flagler. His father was in the business of peddling medicine throughout western New York. The elder Rockefeller had many other pursuits in life and his large family was never poverty stricken. One brother, William Avery, Jr., born in 1841, was also among Flagler's acquaintances and later became associated with his brother and Flagler in what would become the Standard Oil Company.

John's mother, Eliza, perhaps had more influence over the child than did his father largely because of the latter's frequent absences from home. Eliza Rockefeller was stern with her children in their guidance and discipline. The boy grew to be more like his mother than any of the other children. The resemblance pleased her, for he had been named for her father, John Davison.

As a boy, John D. Rockefeller was thorough in everything he did. The story is told about how cautiously he played checkers. He would ponder a move at great length, and never let anyone hurry him in making a decision. When urged by an opponent to move more rapidly, he always let it be known that he was playing the game to win and not to lose; therefore; to him time was of minor consequence in the game. Certainly that instinct, so early seen in his character, stayed with him throughout his life.

In 1850, the Rockefeller family moved to Owego, New York, which was not far from their previous home. There were financial reverses from time to time but John and William were given the advantages of what educational training they could get in the village. Not only did the children attend school, but they all were required to attend Sunday school and church. Religion was a passion with Eliza Rockefeller. They were members of the Baptist Church and John subsequently leaned strongly in its favor. The children were taught to contribute regularly to their church, a habit which young John never forgot. This training perhaps had a great deal to do with his later program of philanthropy.

In 1853, the elder Rockefeller sought greener pastures and turned his attention westward. Selling medicine flourished in frontier places where trained physicians were few in number. He moved to the fringe of the Western Reserve and settled in Cleveland, Ohio. As a lad of 14, John entered Cleveland schools that fall and among his friends was Mark Hanna, son of a prosperous grocer, Leonard

Hanna. Hanna was to become a leading politician, first in Ohio and then in national politics.

John D. Rockefeller graduated from high school in 1855, but did not go to college. His mother had hoped he could go to Western Reserve but his father felt that practical experience would be of more value to him in later life. For three months, John attended a commercial college in Cleveland. He then began to look for employment but since business was bad in 1855, getting a job was no easy matter. Finally he found employment with Hewitt and Tuttle, commission merchants and produce shippers. This was the beginning of his steady rise to the top.

During the time that Henry Flagler was dealing in grain and salt, the petroleum industry in America was making rapid strides. In the states of Pennsylvania, Ohio, Kentucky, and what was later West Virginia, traces of petroleum were discovered on the surface of springs and streams. Some time later, speculators drilling for salt found the dark green, evil-smelling substance. Since oil and salt do not mix, some salt wells were abandoned because of the abundance of crude petroleum. Later, the abandoned salt wells became productive oil wells.

As more and more crude oil appeared, speculators wondered if some real value might be derived from it. In Burkesville, Kentucky, where oil was found in abundance, it was first used for medicinal purposes. "American Medicinal Oil," used as a liniment or rubbing oil, was bottled and sold in the area where it was found in the East, and later even in Europe. The fluid was also used for lamps in shops, factories, and later in homes. Crude oil was found to give good light and before long, streets were illuminated by it. More and more uses were made of petroleum and the demand for it increased. In western Pennsylvania, where petroleum was found in great abundance, the substance was called "Seneca Oil" named for the Seneca Indians who inhabited the region. It was in this section where most of the oil was discovered prior to 1845 in a little stream known as Oil Creek which emptied into the Allegheny River. In this area, boom towns like Titusville and Oil City sprang up.

Until this time, tallow candles, beeswax, and whale oil had been used for lighting purposes. With the decline of whale fisheries, the price for whale oil was exceedingly high by 1850. Lard oil was found only in small quantities; in fact, there was an increasing shortage of oil not only in the United States but all over the world. In the face of this shortage there was increasing demand for more oil. Many new machines were in use which required oil. New railroads were constructed and steamboats were plying more and more of the country's rivers. All these facilities made demands on the small supply of oil in America.

Prior to 1860, there were many advances in the field of petroleum. Samuel M. Kier, who owned salt wells in western Pennsylvania, near Pittsburgh, in the late 1840s, was one of the earliest pioneers. Like many other salt men he grew tired of the smelly green substance which came in such abundance from his salt well. It was such a nuisance that in 1849, he thought of selling it as medicine. His wife, a consumptive, had several bottles of an oil sent from Kentucky. Kier compared the bottled medicine with the substance he was getting from his salt wells. It seemed to be identical. He asked his wife to use the local product rather than the Kentucky oil which her doctor had prescribed. It had the same results and Kier opened a business in nearby Pittsburgh where the curative spirit was bottled and sold. These eight ounce bottles of "Kier's Petroleum" were selling widely by 1850. They were used chiefly as a liniment, but were also recommended for a number of other things including consumption, bronchitis, liver complaints, and cholera morbus. Kier also distilled small quantities of petroleum to use as an illuminant and on the by-products of petroleum. There is little doubt that Samuel M. Kier was the first man to test the possibility of refining oil. He hit upon this process in 1849 after consultation with a chemist in Philadelphia.

Another person to become actively engaged in the development of raw petroleum was George H. Bissell. A graduate of Dartmouth College, he was practicing law in New York. By chance, Bissell visited Hanover, New Hampshire in the fall of 1853. While there, he saw a small bottle of petroleum in the office of Doctor Dixi Crosby of the Dartmouth Medical School and became interested in petroleum after talking with Professor Crosby about its possibilities.

In the fall of 1854, Bissell and his law partner bought about 105 acres of oil lands in the Titusville area. On December 30 of that year they organized the Pennsylvania Rock Oil Company, the first company of its kind in America. The newly organized oil company sent a small quantity of surface petroleum to a noted Yale chemist, Benjamin Silliman, Jr., for analysis. In the spring of 1855, Silliman's report emphasized the usefulness of oil as an illuminant and a lubricant. The findings further stated that many valuable products could be manufactured from it and mentioned many uses for the refined substance. The report also explained how oil was to be refined. Before Bissell could get financial backing and make preparations to drill for oil, that feat was accomplished by Edwin L. Drake, a 38 year-old jack-of-all-trades. Drake went to Titusville in 1857 with the financial support of James M. Townshend, an Eastern banker. With no practical experience in drilling, Drake hired several men and in August 1859, they struck oil. Drake had tapped the subterranean supply of petroleum in a section that was already known for its surface oil. The opening of this well meant that petroleum could now be secured in large quantities. Few men knew much about oil and the refining process, but there were many who were anxious to learn. Many new wells were opened along Oil Creek and the Allegheny River in western Pennsylvania during the early 1860s. An even great expansion of the industry was soon under way.

The oil regions of western Pennsylvania became a center of bustle and activity. Oil men and persons connected indirectly with the industry made money fast. Manufacturers of wooden tanks for oil receptacles made fortunes. Teamsters who drove the wagons carrying barrels of oil out of the oil regions became rich. Traffic on the Allegheny River grew so rapidly that it could hardly take care of the accelerated activity. By 1863, a railroad was extended into Titusville and by 1865, Oil City was supplied with rail service.

Other places also felt the impact of the oil boom. Pithole, Pennsylvania, was engulfed in the tide of prosperity by 1865. In ten months, a field there was producing over 10,000 barrels of petroleum a day. The Civil War had just ended and many returning soldiers were anxious for a chance to find some of the "black gold". Persistent rumors about its value had reached the Union soldiers as the war was drawing to a close. Hundreds of them joined other oil enthusiasts in Pithole. Within a year, the place had grown from a village to a town of 6,000 inhabitants. Pine shanties and oil derricks silhouetted the sky. Among the newcomers were whiskey sellers, horse traders, and deadbeats. Everyone was there for only one purpose – to get rich quick.

Many hardships awaited the newcomers –fluctuation of prices, speculation and discrimination by the railroads.

Prosperity soon spilled across the neighboring borders of New York and Ohio, especially into Cleveland, where people became oil-conscious. Because of good transportation facilities, oil was soon being shipped there for refinement and then on to other places for sale. By 1865, Cleveland had about 30 refineries and more were being built. Located on the southern shore of Lake Erie, and connected with other important points by rail, the city was destined to become an outstanding petroleum center. By 1864, pipe lines were used to send oil out of the oil regions to nearby refining and marketing facilities.

This was a great improvement in the transporting of oil. The teamsters, who had carried large portions of the petroleum to the refineries before 1864, were through. Railroads and pipelines soon became the chief mediums of transportation for unrefined oil.

During the 1860s, the fabulous story of oil spread into other sections of the country as well. Henry Flagler, working hard at his grain business and later in his salt venture, did not have much time to think about oil and its possibilities. It no doubt aroused his curiosity, as it did that of John D. Rockefeller and other get-rich-quick seekers. The first connection Rockefeller had with oil was in 1862, the year in which Flagler went to Saginaw to invest in a salt mine.

In 1862, Rockefeller and his partner in the grain business, Maurice B. Clark, backed Samuel Andrews, an Englishman, in starting a refinery in Cleveland. The move was a gamble for Rockefeller because he knew very little about either Samuel Andrews or the oil business. The first loan was for $4,000. Andrews soon proved his ability. A genius in mechanics, Andrews devised a new process for refining oil. As a result, Rockefeller and Clark poured more capital into the refinery. Rockefeller continued to invest more heavily in the oil business. When business differences came between them, Rockefeller decided to pull out of the grain partnership. Since Maurice Clark was a partner with Andrews in the oil business, Rockefeller gave his half in the grain business, plus $72,000 in cash, for Clark's share in the refining company.

The new oil firm of Rockefeller and Andrews was one of the largest in the United States. Andrews knew the mechanics of the refining business and Rockefeller had a flair for buying and selling. While 25 year-old John D. Rockefeller was teaming up with Samuel Andrews in the oil refining business, Henry Flagler was moving to Cleveland with hopes of remaking his fortune after the Saginaw salt debacle.

Rockefeller was caught up in the rising tide of prosperity and it was not long before Flagler was to share this success. By January 1866, Rockefeller and Andrews had a business worth $1,200,000 with 37 workers and a capacity of 505 barrels a day. This was more than twice the output of any of their competitors.

In 1866, Rockefeller and Flagler had a chance to renew their acquaintance. They both had offices in the Sexton Building and often talked of the days when Flagler had shipped grain from Bellevue to Rockefeller in Cleveland. Over time, their association became more friendly. Since they lived on the same street, they frequently walked home together, sharing stories of the day's happenings in their respective offices. Grain did not have much of an attraction for Rockefeller, although Flagler thought well of the business because he was in the process of making money from it. At 36, Flagler had black hair and a closely cropped mustache. His eyes were dark and he possessed a magnetic personality. His passion for wealth was equal to that of Rockefeller. In business, both men were determined and untiring in their efforts. Neither would be denied success.

Rockefeller and Andrews began to think of expansion. Early in 1866, John's brother William Rockefeller was taken into the partnership and was sent to New York to establish an office there. Andrews superintended the refinery while John D. Rockefeller directed the organization. In the second year of their business, they sold more than $2,000,000 worth of oil and there was still room for expansion. With more capital, there could be a much larger output. Rockefeller had great faith in the future of the industry and by 1866, rapid development was being made in the field of petroleum. The invention of a more efficient refining: the use of torpedoes in drilling, replacement of the clumsy flat car with its wooden tubs by the tank-car, and regular use of pipelines to transport petroleum from the wells to the railroads, modernized the process. Rockefeller, who was among the first to realize the situation, began to look for additional capital. Rockefeller wanted Henry Flagler to join him but Flagler did not have the capital which Rockefeller needed to feed the growing business. Flagler told Rockefeller about Stephen V. Harkness, his wife's first cousin, who had made a fortune in the liquor business and who had a flair for speculation and uncertainty.

Within an hour, Harkness agreed to put $100,000 in the business with the understanding that Flagler should have complete control of the Harkness investment. Rockefeller was thoroughly familiar with Flagler's ability as a businessman and had already talked with him about joining the firm. Flagler was doing well in the grain business, but at his cousin's insistence was delighted to enter the oil company with Rockefeller. With Flagler in the business, Rockefeller tapped the Harkness treasury chest several times later and never failed to get the money he wanted.

In 1867, the partnership of Rockefeller, Andrews and Flagler was formed. Stephen Harkness remained a silent partner in the new firm. Flagler worked well with Rockefeller in the organizing and handling of the business. William Rockefeller, who was in New York, did little of the partnership's planning. Samuel Andrews remained busy superintending the refinery. On March 4 and 5, 1867, the new firm advertised its product in the *Cleveland Leader*. The new firm also announced its office in Cleveland at the Case Building and in New York at 181 Pearl Street:

> "Our readers will notice by the advertisement in another column, that the old and reliable firm of Rockefeller and Andrew has undergone a change, and now appears under the new title of Rockefeller, Andrews and Flagler.
>
> This firm is one of the oldest in the refining business and their trade already a mammoth one, is still further enlarged by the recent change; so that with their New York House, their establishment is one of the largest in the United States. Among the many oil refining enterprises, this seems to be one of the most successful; its heavy capital and consummate management, having kept it clear of the many shoals upon which oil refining houses have so often been stranded."

For the next 15 years, Flagler was Rockefeller's strongest and closest associate. In his *Random Reminiscences of Men and Events: Autobiography, (1909)* Rockefeller frankly discusses his warm friendship with Flagler: it was a "friendship founded on business rather than a business founded on friendship." For years the two men worked together in the same office, they usually got together and did their planning for days to come. Though Flagler was nine years older than Rockefeller, there seemed to be perfect understanding between them.

The Flaglers and Rockefellers lived on Euclid Avenue where most of Cleveland's wealthiest citizens lived in spacious homes surrounded by beautiful lawns and well-kept flower beds. In view of Lake Erie, it was also the home to railroad builder Amasa Stone, the banker Stillman Witt and the politician Henry B. Payne.

Rockefeller's home was one of the most pretentious on the avenue.

Flagler took an active part in the business life of the city, but engaged in none of the social activities. His religious activities were limited because of his wife's increasingly poor health. It was said that for the last 17 years of Mary's life, from 1864 to 1881, Henry Flagler spent only two evenings away from home. He found diversion from business in reading aloud to his wife. His children also claimed much of his time. He was a member of the Cleveland Board of Trade and the Manufacturers Association of Cleveland, but neither took much time away from his family or his business. Two years after the Civil War was over, he urged the Board of Trade to donate money to help destitute people of the South, especially those in Georgia. On December 2, 1867, he was elected one of the 73 delegates from Cleveland to attend the National Manufacturers Convention to be held in the same city.

The new firm of Rockefeller, Andrews and Flagler was a thriving business from the start. Among Flagler's duties was the drawing up of contracts. He always did this well despite the fact that he had no formal legal training. Since the intent and purpose of the contract was always stated accurately and clearly, Rockefeller believed that Flagler had more common sense than almost anyone else. Another of his activities included the construction of new refineries. Flagler insisted on putting up sound structures and would not allow a flimsy shack to be built. As John D. Rockefeller later stated,

> "Everyone was so afraid that the oil would disappear and that the money expended in building would be a loss that the meanest and cheapest buildings were erected for use as refineries. This was the sort of thing Mr. Flagler objected to. While he had to admit that it was possible the oil supply might fail and that the risks of the trade were great, he always believed that if we went into the oil business at all, we should do the work as well as we knew how; that everything should be solid and substantial; and that nothing should be left undone to produce the finest results."

The new firm expanded its business widely when William Rockefeller opened up European markets and sold a large amount of oil abroad. When Flagler went into the business they were refining about 500 barrels each day. Two years later they were shipping 1,500 barrels of refined oil and 3,000 barrels of crude oil a day.

Flagler's most important contribution to the business was in the field of freight-rate negotiations. He took over that task as soon as he joined Rockefeller, realizing that transportation continued to be one of the biggest obstacles facing refiners. Any refiner who had the advantage in the transportation business usually had the advantage in the petroleum industry, so he worked to outmaneuver the other refiners. Pipe lines and water transportation were utilized for bulk transportation but not as extensively as railroads.

In the late 1860s, there were three different railroads systems serving the oil regions. The Atlantic and Great Western, which in 1868 was absorbed by Jay Gould into his Erie System, shuttled into the oil regions at Titusville and Franklin. The second railroad, the Lake Shore and Michigan Southern, which later became a part of the New York Central, tapped the regions at Oil City. The Pennsylvania was the third road reaching into the petroleum-producing area. It controlled the Allegheny Valley Railroad and the Philadelphia and Erie which served Franklin and Titusville. All three of these railroad systems made great profits from oil traffic and competition among them was vigorous.

Jay Gould's Erie System was the first railroad to favor Rockefeller, Andrews and Flagler with special rates and rebates. This was done because Gould wanted to divert all the crude oil shipments to the Cleveland market. Gould also favored two other Cleveland refineries at this time. As chief negotiator, Flagler also began to bargain very early with the Lake Shore and Michigan Southern Railroad. This was one of the few roads which brought crude petroleum from the oil regions to Cleveland where it could be refined and easily routed on to New York by the Lake Shore-New York Central route. J. H. Devereux became vice-president and general manager of the Lake Shore in 1868 and Flagler very soon found favor with the former Civil War general.

Flagler was, without doubt, one of the pioneers in the practice of rebates. Because of Flagler's efforts, his firm began to receive greater concessions from the Lake Shore as one railroad was played against the other until they became the favored refiners in Cleveland. As their volume of shipping increased, their rebates grew. When other refiners complained, as they often did, and petitioned for equal treatment, their requests were usually denied. The railroads told them if they would ship as much oil as Rockefeller, Andrews and Flagler, they would be given the same rebates. To the refiners it was a simple case of the survival of the fittest. The era of ruthless competitive warfare began and the newly-formed Standard Oil was destined to win the race. They carefully studied the methods which Western Union Telegraph Company had used in forming its combination and watched the methods used by the railroads in the process of combining and forming large systems. The idea of the formation of the Standard Oil Company began in the following way. Flagler first mentioned to Rockefeller the possibility of combining with smaller refineries one morning as they were walking to work. Rockefeller thought about the idea and replied, "Yes, Henry, I'd like to combine some of these refineries with ours. The business would be much more simple. But how are you going to determine the unit of valuation? How are you going to find a yardstick to measure the value?" In a few minutes Flagler answered, "John, I'll find a yardstick."

By 1869, Rockefeller, Andrews and Flagler had outdistanced all the other refineries in Cleveland. In all of their early purchases, Flagler used his "yardstick". He determined the value of the refinery and set the price which he and Rockefeller would pay for it. His aggressiveness often caught the seller off guard and the "bargains" he obtained on his purchases were outstanding.

Rockefeller later stated that Flagler was always on the active side of every question, and that his energy was responsible for the rapid growth and progress of the partnership, and later for the Standard Oil Company. Said Rockefeller, "His courage in acting up to his beliefs laid strong foundations for later years."

Historians have concluded that Flagler's genius was essential to the growth of Standard Oil:

- Allan Nevins commented that "next to John D. Rockefeller," Flagler counted for most in the oil industry.
- John T. Flynn maintained that Flagler did a great deal of Rockefeller's thinking, and that the "two men were admirably suited to each other," and that Flagler, "a bold, unscrupulous self-seeker… could be relied upon to propose the needful course…"
- John Winkler believe that Flagler was "fully as capable an organizer" as Rockefeller and did most for the rapidly expanding monopoly.
- Ida M. Tarbell, journalist and "muckraker", declared that when the Standard Oil Company was formed Flagler, next to Rockefeller, was the strongest man in the firm. Miss Tarbell believed that he "had no scruples to make him hesitate over the ethical quality of a contract which was advantageous." Tarbell's "*The History of the Standard Oil Company*" documented the aggressive techniques the company used to roll over whoever got in its way.
- In 1911, the Supreme Court found Standard Oil in violation of the Sherman Antitrust Act and ordered it broken into 34 separate companies.

But in the 19th century, Standard Oil continued to expand by merger, acquisition and consolidation. By 1878, Standard Oil controlled most of the pipe lines carry petroleum from oil-producing regions. In just four years, Rockefeller and Flagler's Standard Oil Company controlled 95% of the country's petroleum industry. The Company became a household word throughout the world. It was spread through Europe, the Middle East, India, Africa and China. Its monopoly obtained franchises from kings, emperors, mandarins and warlords. The Standard Oil logo was familiar in every city and village of Europe, Asia and Africa.

When Flagler relocated to New York City in 1877, he gradually separated himself from the leadership of Standard Oil. After Mary Flagler died in 1881, Flagler's influence steadily diminished in Standard Oil but he remained the second largest stockholder after John D. Rockefeller. By the time Standard Oil was dissolved in 1911, Henry Flagler was an extraordinarily wealthy former founder and stockholder. His subsequent interests in Florida completely replaced his attachments to the Standard Oil Company.

Florida's population in 1880 was 270,000 people, of whom 40,000 lived in the long-settled northeast coast between Jacksonville and St. Augustine. Today, the chief method of traveling to Florida is, of course, by air or highway. Although airlines have been critical to Florida's tourism enterprises, contrary to the popular view, the airlines did not develop the original tourism market for Florida. That distinction should go to Henry Flagler, when he took his second wife on a honeymoon to Jacksonville and then farther south to the seaside village of St. Augustine, (the oldest permanent European settlement in the United States). Flagler loved the breathtaking expanse of sea and shore, and enjoyed the clear skies and balmy weather when most of the rest of the country's residents (then concentrated in the northeast) were locked in by ice and snow.

St. Augustine had been used by the infirm and elderly even before the Civil War but wealthy northerners were just beginning to discover its balmy weather at the end of the nineteenth century. While the Flaglers stayed at the new six-story San Marco Hotel they were surprised at the lack of large hotels and other real estate development. Flagler's interest in St. Augustine was greeted with great interest in financial circles of the nation. At the time, Flagler was as famous as Rockefeller as a world-renowned financier.

On June 5, 1883, Henry Morrison Flagler and Ida Alice Shourds were married at the Madison Avenue Methodist Church in New York City. Miss Shourds had been a nursing attendant for his first wife. They set up housekeeping at the house at 685 Fifth Avenue but the new bride was not welcomed by the Flagler family nor by young Harry. The newly married couple delayed their honeymoon until December 1883 in St. Augustine. Because of a severe cold wave in New York, the Flaglers remained in Florida until March 1, 1884. They returned to Florida in February 1885 and Henry decided to build a new hotel in St. Augustine. He met Franklin W. Smith, a Boston architect whose St. Augustine winter home, the Villa Zorayda, was one of the first cast-in-place concrete buildings in the United States. It was built with a new kind of material made from a mixture of cement and coquina, a soft whitish rock consisting of sea shell and coral.

Because Flagler hated cold weather, he planned a belated honeymoon in Florida in December, 1883. The trip from New York to Jacksonville took 90 hours because of the different gauges of railroad tracks along the way. In 1870, *Harper's Weekly* reported:

"There are two ways of getting to Jacksonville (from Savannah) and whichever you choose you will be sorry to have not taken the other. There is the night train by railroad, which brings you to Jacksonville in about 16 hours; and there is the steamboat line, which goes inland nearly wall the way, and which may land you in a day, or you may run aground and remain on board for a week."

The Jacksonville *News-Herald* reported an interview with Henry Flagler on June 20, 1887,

"I have two stories to tell to every one who asks me my reasons for building the Ponce de Leon Hotel…

I was coming downtown in an El road car in New York recently when a friend said to me, "Flagler, I was asked the other day why you were building that hotel in St. Augustine and replied that you had been looking around for several years for a place to make a fool of yourself in, and at last selected St. Augustine as the spot."

The other story that I used to illustrate my position is this: There was once a good old church member who had lived a correct life, until well advanced in years he got on a spree. While in this state he met his good pastor. After being roundly upbraided for his condition, he replied, "I have been giving all my days to the Lord hithereto, and now I'm taking one for myself." This is somewhat my case. For 14 years I have devoted my time exclusively to business, now I am pleasing myself."

In that same newspaper story, Flagler explained that he intended to build the best hotel possible:

> "I am not a hotel builder. I have just completed an office building for the Standard Oil Company in New York that cost over a million dollars. But the Ponce de Leon is an altogether different affair. I want something to last all time to come and have no doubt made the walls much more expensive than necessary, but I had much rather spend $50,000 too much than $50,000 too little. I take a great deal of pride in it, and watch its progress with much interest. I will, however, have a hotel that suits me in every respect, and one that I can thoroughly enjoy, cost what it may. I tell my friends that when they stop at the Ponce de Leon it will cost them a good deal of money, but guarantee them that they will get its full return in value."

One event that might have heightened his interest was the anniversary celebration in March, 1885 of the landing of Ponce de Leon. Flagler later recalled the difficulty of deciding on the design of his new Ponce de Leon Hotel. "Here was St. Augustine, the oldest city in the United States. How to build a hotel to meet the requirements of nineteenth century America and have it in keeping with the character of the place - that was my hardest problem."

Flagler hired two young architects from McKim, Mead and White: John M. Carrere and Thomas Hastings to design his new hotel. Hasting's father, a Presbyterian minister, was a close friend of Flagler. Later, Carrere & Hastings would design more than 600 buildings including the New York Public Library and the U.S. House and Senate Office Building in Washington. The 540-room Ponce de Leon Hotel opened on January 10, 1888 on a five-acre lot with Spanish Renaissance architecture. On opening day, Flagler's invited guests arrived on the first plush vestibule train ever to arrive in St. Augustine. That evening, Mr. and Mrs. Flagler entertained the hotel's architects, builders, artists and railroad executives. The first impression of the Ponce de Leon was of size, since the mammoth structure covered most of its five-acre lot. The building was only four stories high but it was large and extensive. Inside the front gate was the beautifully landscaped 10,000 square foot interior court containing a large fountain with a grand entrance to the rotunda. The building's design and ornamentation embodied the style of Spanish Renaissance architecture.

The heartbeat of the hotel was in the spacious rotunda. Its great dome was supported by massive oak columns and its floor was brilliant with inlaid colored mosaics. The architects tried to capture the spirit of Old Spain with allegorical representations of the four elements: fire, water, air, earth and four figures: adventure, discovery, conquest and civilization. Behind the dome of the rotunda was the oval-shaped dining hall seating 700 with stained glass windows, highly polished floors and enormous columns of antique oak. The ceiling art representing the history of St. Augustine was painted by Virgilio Tojetti, one of the foremost artists of the day.

The success of the design of the Ponce de Leon is recorded by the noted Gilded Age author, Henry James in his 1907 book, *The American Scene*. James writes, "The Ponce de Leon, for that matter, comes as close as near producing, all by itself, the illusion of romance as a highly modern, a most cleverly-constructed and smoothly-administered great modern caravansery can come…and is, in all sorts of ways and in the highest sense of the word, the most 'amusing' of hotels."

The hotel had electric lights, steam heat, private parlors, reading and game rooms, exquisite draperies, imported rosewood, walnut and mahogany furniture and Brussels carpet. Since standards of the day deemed public bathrooms sufficient, the hotel originally had only one private bathroom- in Flagler's suite. Almost immediately it became necessary to add private bathrooms to the hotel rooms.

Among the hundreds of guests were Mrs. Ulysses S. Grant, Frederick Vanderbilt and William R. Rockefeller. During its first five years, the Ponce de Leon was the most exclusive winter palace resort in the United States. Its guests included Hamilton Disston, the nation's largest landowner; Vice President Levi P. Morton; Governor Roswell Flower of New York; Chauncey Depew; Charles A. Dana of New York Sun; and President Grover Cleveland who later visited the hotel in 1889, 1893, 1899, 1903 and 1905. Four other presidents also visited the hotel including William McKinley, who was then governor of Ohio in 1895; Theodore Roosevelt in 1905; Warren G. Harding in 1921; and many years later Vice President Lyndon B. Johnson in 1963.

The Ponce de Leon Hotel was the center of formal entertainment. One of these affairs was the Hermitage Ball held in 1892 to raise money for the restoration of Andrew Jackson's Tennessee home. There were swimming exhibitions at the Casino pool, horsemanship tournaments, bicycling and tennis. In 1895, the first golf links were laid on the Fort Marian green and there was great interest among the winter guests in golf equipment and professional instruction. In a manifestation of Jim Crow racism, guests would sometimes attend cake walks performed by the Negro bellhops and waiters. The event would begin with a "buck dance", a brisk double-shuffle by one black performer followed by singing and the cake walk itself. Well-dressed white couples would then stroll in time to the music and vie for prizes awarded by a panel of judges of their peers. Later, cake walks were sometimes replaced by black-faced minstrel shows.

In order to attract northern vacationers so soon after the Civil War and Reconstruction, Florida had to remake its image. After all, Florida was the third state, after South Carolina and Mississippi to secede from the Union and join the Confederate States of America. In the years after the Civil War, U.S. federal officers visiting the South observed that the feeling toward northerners in Georgia, South Carolina and Florida was bitter and hostile. After the Civil War, the Ku Klux Klan and other terrorist organizations brutalized the newly-freed former slaves, free black landowners and officeholders with lynchings, murders and arson. As late as 1873, *Harper's Weekly* reported that Florida was "suited for cultivation as a resort… but for its ceaseless political disturbances…" Northern reporters stated that Floridian's intolerance would drive away potential investment and reduce the state to perpetual wasteland. In St. Augustine, Henry Flagler's choice of Spanish Renaissance Revival design for his hotels was not accidental. It solidified the city's claim to Spanish heritage and helped to stimulate tourism by erasing memories of Florida's participation on the Confederate side of the brutal Civil War conflict. Founded in 1565, St. Augustine had Spanish origins and was known as "the Ancient City". Flagler could, therefore, be a modern-day Ponce de Leon rather than a carpetbagger and promote Florida as a more desirable vacation destination for Northerners.

The George Maynard paintings and murals "Adventure, Discovery, Conquest and Civilization" in the ceiling of the Ponce de Leon's rotunda and dining room reflected the history of Spanish Florida, not the history of slavery or of racist sectional strife. There was no place in this selective history for slaveholders and secessionists but only dashing explorers. The "Change of Flags" segment of a local festival included Spanish, French, English and American flags but not the Confederate flag.

The management of the Ponce de Leon had to provide housing for its hotel employees. Behind the main dining hall was a large building which contained the kitchen, workshops, living quarters for the hotel's white employees and several employee dining rooms. A quarter of a mile away on Cordova Street, black males were housed in the so-called "colored barracks" while black women lived in the large laundry building near the railroad depot. A variety of other skilled employees worked in the Flagler hotels: plumbers, gardeners, chefs, musicians, engineers and two Pinkerton detectives to protect wealthy guests from "bunko" artists. Most of these employees worked in northern hotels in the summer and in southern resorts in the winter.

In 1899, Flagler built seven studios in the rear of the Ponce de Leon which were occupied by famous New England painters whose landscapes promoted Florida to the rest of the country. The weekly receptions held by the artists were among the social highlights of the winter season.

No sooner did the Ponce de Leon Hotel open than Flagler realized that the market would require a companion hotel catering to a more frugal clientele and to accommodate the overflow from the Ponce de Leon. Flagler again hired Carrere & Hastings to design the Hotel Alcazar (an Arabic word meaning "royal castle") and its Casino across the street from the Ponce de Leon. Flagler's army of laborers crossed King Street and began construction of the Alcazar. The site had been cleared by the removal of the Olivet Methodist Church, the demolition of the San Marco roller-skating rink building and the landfill of the creek bed on the site. The Alcazar was smaller than the Ponce de Leon. The structure, 250 feet by 400 feet, was four stories high and was built around a court and arcades with stores, restaurants, shops and salons. The façade was a reproduction of the famous Alcazar in Seville, Spain.

The Alcazar, while not as elaborate as the Ponce de Leon, nevertheless had some unique features such as the Casino and Baths which were opened in early February 1889. In anticipation of the spa development of one hundred years later, Flagler incorporated the following:

- A Turkish bath (the Senate) with dry heat of 160°-180° Fahrenheit where patrons sat on marble tiers wrapped in togas to endure the heat. Flagler hired a Turkish attendant from Chicago's Palmer House Hotel to supervise the baths. Hotel advertising touted the baths as cure-alls for heart disease, as well as for gout, rheumatism, liver and kidney diseases, neurasthenia and obesity. Patrons would enter the baths from the hotel or the Casino and go to one of forty cubicle dressing rooms to disrobe. Then they would follow a regime prescribed by their physician or by the staff, which might involve being sprayed from a hose and given a shampoo followed by a steam soak in the Russian bath, where a variety of jets of water would be sprayed; then back to the steam room, and finally, a quick cold plunge in the center of the bath area. Afterwards, the guest would probably have a massage and a glass of Clarendon Springs mineral water.

- The Baths also contained a small well-furnished gymnasium where they could exercise amid the Carrere & Hastings version of the modern fitness center. There were dumb-bells, pulleys, weights, Indian clubs, punching bags, parallel and horizontal bars and oriental rugs serving as mats. Women could use the Baths and gymnasium at scheduled times when female attendants supervised the treatments.

The Casino building was a huge structure that contained a swimming pool 120 feet long and 50 feet wide, ranging in depth from 3 feet to more than 12 feet. Light was provided in the daytime from the glassed-over roof above the pool. In the evening, one thousand electric lights illuminated the interior. One floor above, completely encircling the pool area, was the ballroom with its highly-polished floor.

The water in the pool came from an artesan well sunk 1,400 feet deep into the Florida aquifer. While the water's natural temperature was above eighty degrees, it was permeated with sulphur which, despite aeration, gave off a "rotten-egg" smell. The eastern end of the pool was for the men while the western end for women was partitioned off so that those too modest to swim in public could take a dip in private.

Flagler was proud of the Alcazar and described it as follows:

> "(It) will furnish superior accommodations for those who do not wish to stay at the other hotel. Amusements will be provided and the vicinity of the hotel made as attractive as possible. The Methodist Church, which I am constructing across

the avenue on the north, will be the finest church edifice south of the Potomac. The Casa Monica (a hotel designed by Franklin Smith, later purchased by Flagler and renamed the Cordova) is very near and it is a handsome structure. These, with the big hotel (Ponce de Leon) and the Alcazar, will make a beautiful group."

Flagler's operational policy was a forerunner of the "loss leader" theory of hotel management. He believed that a fine hotel or restaurant was bound to lose a certain amount of money before it established itself as a place of bona-fide quality. In the 1890s, as the Ponce continued to operate at high occupancies, a new hotel manager decided to economize. He wired Flagler for permission to discharge the costly French chef and an equally costly dance band. Flagler wired back, "Hire another cook and two more of the best orchestras."

By the early 1890s, Henry Flagler was St. Augustine's greatest benefactor. He built a modern hospital and contributed money toward the building of a City Hall and an African-American school. He donated money to install electric lights, pave streets, lay sewers, build railroad car shops and homes for his employees. He was 60 years old and appeared to be the beneficiary of Ponce de Leon's supposed fountain-of-youth. His greatest accomplishments still lay ahead of him.

For 15 years after the Civil War, there was no new railroad construction in Florida. By 1884, the few railroads along Florida's Atlantic coast each had a different track width and therefore, none of the early railroads could interchange rolling stock. In order to service his planned resorts, Flagler needed standardized track and dependable railroad service. With characteristically direct action, Flagler purchased the Jacksonville, St. Augustine & Halifax River Railroad and had the track between Jacksonville and St. Augustine widened to standard gauge. Subsequently he acquired the St. Augustine and Palatka Railroad, the St. Johns Railroad and the logging road to Daytona. After standard gauge tracks were laid along these routes, Flagler's entire railroad was as modern as could be found anywhere in the South. Flagler's business acumen continued to lead him to southern Florida along the Atlantic coast.

Near Daytona, Flagler bought the Ormond Beach Hotel in 1890. He enlarged the building to 150 rooms, beautified the grounds and constructed a new 18-hole golf course. In 1890, Daytona Beach was the southern terminus of all standard gauge rail on the East coast. At that time, it was possible to board a Pullman in New York City and ride all the way to St. Augustine, Ormond Beach and Daytona Beach without changing trains. For the first time, Flagler became a railroad developer and builder, pushing south through the coastline of eastern Florida to New Smyrna to Rockledge to Eau Gallie. By the end of January 1894, new rail had been constructed to Fort Pierce, 242 miles from Jacksonville. In less than two years, Flagler had built 130 miles of standard gauge railroad.

After two years of study, Flagler obtained a charter from the state of Florida in 1892 authorizing him to build a railroad along the Indian River as far south as Miami. In 1893, the Florida State Legislature awarded 8,000 acres of land for each mile of railroad built south of Daytona Beach. Flagler eventually owned two million acres of Florida land.

Flagler created the Model Land Company which probably did more to build up Florida's east coast than any of his other undertakings. The Model Land Company, under the direction of Henry Plant's former top executive, James E. Ingraham, hired expert agriculturists, horticulturists and stockmen who were well versed on soils, crops and farm production.

Flagler's land policies resulted in the settling of Delray, Deerfield, Dania, Ojus, Peerine, Homestead, Kenansville and Okeechobie as well as Fort Lauderdale, Miami and West Palm Beach.

As the railroad moved south, Flagler did not neglect St. Augustine, buying the Hotel Casa Monica and renaming it the Cordova Hotel. Flagler also donated funds to build the Memorial Presbyterian Church, a hospital and to rebuild the Catholic Cathedral when it burned down. He underwrote the construction of the City Hall, the first installation of electric lights and public water works and the paving of St. Augustine's streets.

In the spring of 1893, Flagler purchased a large tract of land between Lake Worth and the Atlantic Ocean. It was located in what is now Palm Beach County. In 1894, Palm Beach was a barrier island separated from the mainland by an arm of the ocean called Lake Worth. It was named after General William J. Worth who had been sent there before the Civil War to settle Indian uprisings. The lake shores were beautiful with overhanging trees, jungle vines and exotic foliage. One of the first settlers in the late 1870s was Robert R. McCormick, founder of the International Harvester Company. He built a home on Lake Worth with a fabulous tropical garden containing a wide variety of Southern Florida's flowers, shrubs, trees and palms. Meanwhile, Flagler acquired about a half mile of frontage for $45,000 on the mainland which ultimately became West Palm Beach. He broke ground on May 1, 1893 for what was to become the South's largest hotel, the Royal Poinciana.

The story of how Palm Beach got its name is worth recalling. In 1878, the Spanish ship Provindencia, sailing from Trinidad to Spain, sank in a storm off the Florida coast. The residents of the Lake Worth community salvaged the cargo of fledgling coconut palm trees, planted them on the scrubland and adopted the name of Palm Beach. Flagler assembled the parcels of land which formed the nucleus of the new town of West Palm Beach.

In 1893, construction began on the Royal Poinciana Hotel in Palm Beach, after commodore Charles J. Clarke purchased the Coconut Grove House from Elisha Dimick. Clarke's guests were forced to find other accommodations when he leased the entire hotel to Henry Flagler to house one hundred of his upper-level employees. Six months later, the Coconut Grove House burned to the ground and Flagler had to find alternative housing for his employees. One thousand workers built the Royal Poinciana Hotel using 1,400 kegs of nails, 360,000 shingles, 500,000 bricks, 500,000 feet of lumber, 2,400 gallons of paint, 4,000 barrels of lime, 1,200 windows, and 1,800 doors.

On February 11, 1894 the Royal Poinciana Hotel opened with 540 guestrooms on six floors. Flagler expanded the hotel almost immediately after opening increasing its capacity to 1,000 guests. The size of the structure was immense with more than 3 miles of corridors.

In order to build the Royal Poinciana and the Florida East Coast Railway extension at the same time, black workers were brought from the Bahamas. They lived in a segregated camp, called "the Styx" without running water or electricity.

The Royal Poinciana was called the "Queen of Winter Resorts" and was considered the largest resort hotel in the world when it was opened. In the center of the six-story building was a large rotunda from which ran several miles of corridors. There were lounges, parlors, drawing rooms and a casino. The interiors were designed with the utmost care and taste. The building was enlarged in 1899 and again in 1901. Flagler built this palace as a winter playground for America's wealthiest guests, locating it on the main line of his Florida East Coast Railway. Some of these guests were able to park their private railway cars right up to the hotel's entrance. In the first year of operation, with the telephone still a rare luxury, bellmen were obliged to carry message between the front desk and guestrooms by bicycle. Flagler spared no expense to entertain his wealthy patrons including fishing trips out into the Atlantic Ocean. The hotel was the center of social activity for the wealthy upper classes. Approximately 1,400 employees were on duty during the open season, usually from December to April. In addition to the spectacular annual Washington Birthday Ball, there were cake walks, teas, ballroom dances and expensive catered social events. Extensive outdoor activities included two 18-hole golf courses, tennis courts, motor boats, wicker wheelchairs, bicycles and a mule-drawn trolley car to and from the beach. There were two swimming pools, one with "fresh" sulphur water and one with salt water from the ocean.

Unlike his hotels in St. Augustine which were built of stone and coquina, Flagler used wood for the Royal Poinciana Hotel. In season, the Royal Poinciana employed 400 waiters and 287 chambermaids. It had a separate employee dining room for the

lower echelons of hotel staff and another for first officers, a third
dining room for the second officers, a fourth for servants of the
guests, and a fifth for children. The staff had its own orchestra for
their dances and other social functions. The head housekeeper had
a three-room suite. Outdoor activities were very popular at the
Royal Poinciana including golf, tennis, boating, fishing and more.
In an unfortunate manifestation of the racism of the day, African
American bicyclists pedaled white guests seated in attached wicker
chairs called "Afrimobiles".

The hotel contained spacious dining rooms, fancy shops and an
"Ask Mr. Foster" travel office. Outdoor activities included ocean
swimming, boating, tennis, golf and day trips on the hotel's
houseboat. The hotel was so popular that it was expanded in
1899, 1901 and 1929 with new guestrooms, dining rooms and a
new greenhouse restaurant. Some wealthy guests arrived in their
own private Pullman cars which housed their servants during the
vacation.

Karl P. Abbott wrote in *Open For the Season* (Doubleday &
Company, Inc., Garden City, New York 1950):

> "When the Royal Poinciana opened in January
> 1894, additions followed swiftly, until the hotel
> had a thousand guest rooms. It was the largest
> frame strictly resort hotel in the world, and so far
> as I know there has never been another so large.
> The hotel accommodated seventeen hundred and
> fifty guests and required a staff of about twelve
> hundred employees, all of whom were housed
> and fed in a dormitory which was a great hotel
> in itself. There were approximately three hundred

colored waiters, and as they left their dormitory on a sunny day, dressed in their uniforms with snowy white shirt bosoms, they looked like a miniature army advancing upon the hotel. The dining room accommodated two thousand guests at a single sitting, and to quote Ring Lardner: "From one end of the room to the other was a toll call."

Business tycoons, the Newport set, theatrical stars, politicians of the day made the Poinciana a mecca for their winter vacations, and the winter colony round about grew apace; Colonel Bradley built his wonderful gambling Casino; Flagler, his beautiful residence, Whitehall, and the magnificent hotel Breakers on the beach."

Colonial Bradley's Beach Club and Casino was a notorious private club and restaurant with an octagonal gaming room where guards carried machine guns. Flagler disapproved of the gambling but did not shut Bradley down because his hotel guests enjoyed the Club.

The hotel had extensive back-of-the-house boiler rooms, generators, kitchens, laundry and staff housing in separate buildings. An 1894 souvenir brochure showed the layout of the laundry and praised its up-to-date technology. Advanced techniques were also evident in the unique fire escape equipment. Each guestroom was equipped with a rope ladder that allowed guests to be lowered mechanically to the ground level. These ladders had seats and galvanized fixtures with ladder hooks.

After Flagler built the Royal Poinciana, he became a major benefactor of the area. He built houses for his employees and contributed public funds for the construction of West Palm Beach's prominent buildings. He donated a plot of land for a municipal cemetery. He also built the Catholic Church in the city because a large number of his employees were Catholics.

Flagler's second hotel in Palm Beach was the unpretentious Palm Beach Inn, about a quarter mile east of the Royal Poinciana on the Atlantic Coast which was built as an annex for bathers and swimmers. It became as popular as the Poinciana and its name was changed to the Breakers Hotel. It was destroyed by fire in 1903, rebuilt in 1906 and destroyed again by fire in 1925. After Flagler's death, his heirs vowed that this disaster would never happen again. They engaged the famous architectural firm of Schultze & Weaver (who later designed the Waldorf-Astoria, the Pierre and the Sherry-Netherland in New York City) to build a concrete structure reinforced with eleven hundred tons of steel. The owners, determined not to miss the upcoming December-to-May social season, employed some twelve hundred construction workers, who completed the hotel in less than a year. Seventy-two Italian artisans were imported to execute the paintings on the ceilings of the lobby and other first-floor public rooms. From its opening day, December 29, 1926, the Breakers was the resort hotel of choice for the American social set, who arrived in private railroad cars, some for three-to-four month stays. These wealthy guests were accompanied by dozens of steamer trunks, gold-encrusted jewelry cases, lizard-encased golf clubs and a retinue of servants who resided in tiny cubicles equipped with call bells to provide their employers with twenty-four-hour access to their services.

Between the two hotels, Flagler developed a vast park with spectacular landscaping and a miniature railway with cars pulled by donkeys. Serpentine walkways crossed acres of lawn and intersected with hundreds of flower beds and rows of palm trees and Australian pines. In the Roaring Twenties, gentlemen drank bootleg gin and smoked cigars in a gallery overlooking the Circle Dining Room. Guests danced the Charleston till dawn. For a time, a three-to-seven A.M. "nightcap breakfast" was served. But with the stock market crash of 1929, the Breakers' popularity began to wane. During World War II, the Breakers Hotel was converted to a U.S. Army hospital. The Royal Poinciana was demolished by the Flagler System in 1935.

Following the end of World War II, the Breakers struggled to regain its former opulence. Every spring when it closed its doors, the windows were rubbed with soap to keep out the sun, and the furniture was covered with sheets. During the winter season, the room-sized vault lined with boxes that once held an emperor's treasure of emeralds, rubies and diamonds, stood empty. In the abandoned gallery, the paintings of nymphs on the ceiling were peeling; the cracked walls still reeked of stale cigar smoke. By 1970, in an effort to enter the modern world, the hotel added air-conditioning and convention facilities, but it never regained its former glory until the 1990 renovations. The Breakers has long been controlled by the Kenan family, relatives of Mary Lily Kenan, the third wife of Henry Morrison Flagler, and in 1990 they finally committed $75 million to a complete renovation. Among the more recent additions is the Flagler Club, twenty-eight deluxe rooms with special services, including those of a dedicated concierge. There are fourteen tennis courts and two 18-hole golf courses. (The first, completed in 1896, is the oldest in Florida). The beach club has a massive pool, a kiddie pool, beach cabanas and an outdoor and an indoor restaurant. Personal trainers, fitness classes and massages are available.

In 1897, when Ida Alice Flagler was institutionalized for good, Flagler's affair with Mary Lily Kenan was an open secret. On April 9, 1901, nearly two years after he proposed to Mary Lily, a bill was introduced into the Florida State legislature which allowed incurable insanity to be a ground for divorce. In less than a month, the bill was approved by both houses and was signed into law by the governor. It was rumored that the bill's passage cost Flagler twenty thousand dollars in payoffs and bribes.

When Flagler was granted a divorce from Ida Alice in June, he placed $2 million in trust which provided her with an income of $120,000 per year. Seven days after his filing for divorce, Flagler announced his engagement to Mary Lily Kenan. He was seventy-one and she was thirty-four years of age. Their marriage took place on August 24th and Flagler spared no expense to make his new bride happy.

Flagler built a fabulous 55-room Palm Beach mansion, called Whitehall, which was reputed to cost $2.5 million. A reporter for the *New York Herald*, writing in March 1902, described the mansion as "more wonderful than any palace in Europe, grander and more magnificent than any other private dwelling in the world….. the Taj Mahal of North America." Whitehall was a wedding present for his third wife and where the Flaglers spent their winters from 1902 to 1913. The couple entertained lavishly while vacationing at Whitehall and guests stayed in opulent guest suites that were furnished in antique European style.

Then, as now, northern Florida was subject to occasional periods of wintry cold. After an intense cold snap in 1894, Flagler turned his attention farther south. Fort Dallas, an outpost located at the mouth of the Miami River, was built after the outbreak of the

Seminole War in 1836. Julia Tuttle, a friend of John D. Rockefeller, lived there and owned 640 acres of woodlands and marshland bordering the Miami River and Biscayne Bay. Tuttle promised to share half her land with Flagler if he would extend the Florida East Coast Railway to Miami. Flagler agreed and Tuttle then divided her land into small plots, giving every other plot to Flagler, which forced him to purchase her remaining plots in order to secure a contiguous 640 acres of land. Acquiring more land on Biscayne Bay, Flagler extended his railroad in April 1896 to Miami where he built a railway terminal, streets, and a municipal water system. Soon thereafter, Flagler built a new hotel, the grandiose five-story 450-room Royal Palm. Like all Flagler hotels from St. Augustine to Miami, the hotel was constructed of wood and painted yellow with green trim. The Royal Palm had a large swimming pool, a magnificent dining room and a grand ballroom. A smaller hotel, the Biscayne, with 150-rooms was leased and operated year-round. The Great Hurricane of 1926 damaged the 600-room hotel and it was demolished in 1930. Upon the incorporation of the new city, the residents wanted to name the new city "Flagler" in appreciation. Instead, Flagler urged that it be called "Miami", the Indian name for the river that ran through the city.

Most of the laborers in Flagler's workforce were blacks from southern states, the Bahamas and other Caribbean islands. The center of the South Florida black community was Colored Town (later called Overtown) which was created in 1896 in northwest Miami. Blacks were denied equal housing, business opportunities, voting rights and the use of the beaches. But one black construction laborer who worked as a carpenter for Florida's East Coast Railroad recognized the need to provide housing for black workers. Dana Albert Dorsey was the son of former slaves whose formal education was provided at a school run during Reconstruction by the Freedmen's Bureau in

Quitman, Georgia. After moving to Miami in 1897, the talented Dana Dorsey engaged in truck farming but soon began to invest in real estate. He purchased lots for $25 each in Colored Town and constructed one rental house per parcel. He built many of the so-called shotgun houses and rented them out, but never sold any.

According to his daughter Dana Dorsey Chapman, in a 1990 interview, her father's excellent penmanship was the product of his early formal education at the Freedmen's Bureau school. Dorsey's business expanded as far north as Fort Lauderdale. He donated land to the Dade County Public Schools on which the Dorsey High School was built in 1936 in Liberty City. In 1970, its purpose was changed to meet the needs of the adults in the community by becoming the D.A. Dorsey Educational Center. In Overtown, the Dorsey Memorial Library opened on August 13, 1941 on land he donated shortly before his death in 1940. That building was renovated and restored under the direction of my brother, the late Leonard Turkel, a Miami Beach philanthropist and businessman. The first black-owned hotel in Florida was the Dorsey Hotel in Overtown. The hotel placed advertisements in black and white newspapers and was constantly upgraded by Dorsey, including adding hot and cold running water. Marvin Dunn in his landmark book, *Black Miami in the Twentieth Century* (University Press of Florida 1997) reports that,

> "The Dorsey house was always filled with important dinner guests. Some of the white millionaires who visited were awed by Dorsey's accomplishments, achieved under difficult circumstances. Some even went to him for financial help. According to his daughter, during the Depression, Dorsey lent money

to William M. Burdine to keep his department store open. When Dorsey died in 1940, flags were lowered to half-staff all over Miami."

In 1918, Dorsey purchased a 216-acre island sliced from the tip of Miami in 1905 when the government dredged out a sea-lane from Biscayne Bay. His intention was to create a beach resort for blacks because they were forbidden to use all other public beaches. Briefly, the beach he owned became a popular spot for blacks to picnic and bathe. However, the land boom of 1925 skyrocketed property value and he sold the island to the Alton Beach Realty Company owned by Carl Graham Fisher who named it Fisher Island. It is now one of the wealthiest enclaves in the United States.

Flagler was not content with his mainland Florida railroad and hotel operations. He began a venture to extend his holdings southward which included Nassau, Havana and Key West. One of Flagler's first steamboat purchases was the Santa Lucia in 1892 which was refitted for service on the Indian River. She started operation as the A. Nellie Hudson No. 2 built in Pittsburgh for service on the Allegheny River. Flagler purchased the vessel because he needed to get materials to Palm Beach to build his Royal Poinciana Hotel. The Santa Lucia also brought some of the equipment and supplies for the construction of the Royal Palm Hotel in Miami.

A quarantine against yellow fever was established and The Santa Maria was docked at Miami's waterfront where citizens brought various articles for sterilization.

Flagler initiated steamship service from Palm Beach to Nassau. Because of shallow water conditions in the Atlantic Ocean, a long pier was built easterly to reach ocean water depths sufficient for ocean-going vessels without grounding. Proximity to the hotel was necessary so that guests could get to their rooms with only a short walk. In anticipation of hurricane-type weather, a steel and timber trestle-type pier supported by a rock-filled bulkhead was built at a cost of $100,000 in 1897.

Flagler was determined to play a part in the winter tourist trade with the Bahamas. To that end, he acquired the Royal Victoria Hotel. In mid-January 1895, he instituted steamship service with the steamship North Umberland and in late 1897, contracted with the Bahamian government to build a new hotel with 340 rooms to be operated at least 10 weeks each year. He also agreed to provide fast and frequent mail and passenger service between Nassau and the mainland.

The brand new Colonial Hotel soon surpassed the Royal Victoria which was closed after the 1901 season. Flagler's steamship operations were organized as the Florida East Coast Steamship Company whose Vice President was Joseph R. Parrott, a cum laude Yale University Law School graduate. Over the years, Parrot had been president of the FEC Railway and before that had been president of hotel operations. He was Flagler's strong right arm.

Initially, Flagler had doubts about going further south than the Palm Beaches but a severe winter freeze in 1894-1895 convinced him to look further south beyond the Miami area. The first survey of a railroad route to Key West was made in 1866 by civil engineer J.C. Bailey for the International Ocean Telegraph Company. When the Western Union Telegraph Company gained control of the IOT, the survey report came into the possession of Western Union board member Henry Flagler before 1894. In that same year, Flagler made a trip to Cuba with Sir William Van Horne, the well-known American entrepreneur who built the Canadian Pacific Railway and many of the spectacular Canadian Resorts and Hotels. After the Spanish-American War, Van Horne became one of the chief promoters of railway and industrial enterprise in Cuba. After his conversations with Van Horne, Flagler began consideration of a car-ferry link between Key West and the Cuban railroads with connections to Miami.

As early as 1895, Flagler recognized the possibility of developing the Keys and commenced acquiring a number of them including ownership of nearly one-half of Key Largo, the largest island. These islands had been described as "worthless, chaotic fragments of Coral reef, limestone and mangrove swamp." But the soil of many of the Keys was fertile for the growing of pineapples, bananas, limes and some vegetables. The importance of Key West as a port increased after Flagler's failure to dredge Biscayne Bay and make Miami a port city.

With his Miami hotel project well underway, Flagler turned his attention to Key West. As early as the 1850s, developers considered the possibility of a railroad to Key West. South Florida's first U.S. Senator Stephen R. Mallory promoted the project as "America's Gibraltar". But this idea did not gain traction until July 1905 with Henry Flagler's official announcement that he would build the Key West Extension across the Straits of Florida to Key West. He had been thinking about an Overseas Railroad since 1898 at the conclusion of the Spanish-American War. He and his top-level managers commissioned preliminary engineering reports and feasibility surveys. Flagler tried to keep his plans secret so as to prevent inflating the cost of right-of-way acquisition. In fact, the topography of the Florida Keys did not allow many alternatives for locating the railroad line. His project engineers spent a great amount of time and money planning this difficult 156-mile railroad project from Key Largo to Key West.

When the financier was asked how he could possibly build a railroad down to the Keys, he replied, "It is perfectly simple. All you have to do is to build one concrete arch, and then another, and pretty soon you will find yourself in Key West." In 1904, Flagler made the decision to create the Overseas Railroad when he hired J.C. Meredith who was famous for his knowledge of reinforced concrete. Meredith had just completed construction of a massive pier at Tampico for the Mexican government. In 1904, Meredith hired William Julius Krome to survey a route for the Key West Extension from Homestead to Key Largo via Card Point and then to Key Largo via Jewfish Creek, discovering Lake Surprise, which appeared on no maps, while doing so. Krome worked under Meredith for five years and replaced him in 1909. Krome was also a noted horticulturalist and was well-known and when he died on October 2, 1929, his obituary was published in newspapers across the United States.

Aside from the sheer breadth of the project of 156 miles across the Gulf of Mexico, there were good business reasons for the Overseas Railroad. The Spanish-American war of 1898 brought Cuba into close affiliation with the United States. Key West was only 90 miles from Havana. The Panama Canal was about to be built which would place Key West three hundred miles closer than any other Gulf Port for produce, fruit and sugar from all over the Caribbean and from Central and South America.

When bids for construction were called for, only one was received. Its "cost-plus" terms were not acceptable to Flagler. He decided to build the railroad himself under the direction of general manager

Joseph R. Parrott who, when asked by Flagler "Joe, are you sure that railroad can be built?" "Yes, sir, I am sure." Then Flagler is reported to have said "Very well, then. Go to Key West". From Homestead, on the mainland, south to 30-mile long Key Largo, construction was easily accomplished because it was all land-based. On Key Largo three hundred black workers from Florida and the Bahamas hacked out a path through tropical jungle. They were besieged by heat, mosquitoes and sand flies that stung. Alligators and rattlesnakes were a constant menace. All the building materials, food, fresh water and medical supplies had to be transported by barge for three to five thousand laborers.

For the construction activities there were fourteen houseboats accommodating more than a hundred workers each; three floating pile-drivers, eight work boats with derricks and concrete mixers; more than a hundred barges and lighters; thirty gasoline launches and one floating machine shop. All floating equipment was fitted with dynamos to generate electric lights. A fleet of ocean-going vessels carried coal and crushed rock from the mainland and cement from Germany.

On October 17, 1906, a 100-plus miles per hour hurricane hit the construction area and it is estimated that one hundred and thirty men died. One important lesson was learned: workers were no longer to be housed on boats. Wooden barracks were constructed for them on land from then on. Luckily, there were no hurricanes in 1907. During October, twenty-five hundred men were employed and lived in railroad camps as far south as Knights Key, halfway to Key West.

The bulk of the construction work force came from the low-income districts of Philadelphia and New York. Lack of liquor and women created extensive discontent and turnover. While four thousand men were at work during 1907, twenty thousand had been transported to the Keys during the first three years. Most of them quit after their first paycheck and/or were fired after their first big drunk.

The U.S. Government insisted on construction of a certain number of bridges not a solid wall from the mainland to Key West which they feared would shut off tidal flow. Despite labor problems, local opposition and U.S. Government interference, the Key West Extension got built faster than expected. There was enough track laid in the first year so that coal-burning railroads could be used to bring supplies from the mainland. Much of the rolling stock was built on the job: camp cars with sleeping and dining facilities; supply cars; blacksmith-shop cars; machine-shop cars and a big handcar called the "Bull Moose". Six dredges with gasoline engines were put on wheels on a steel track. General Manager Joseph Parrott backed up the engineers with eighty tramp steamers carrying crushed rock, 200,000 tons of coal, plus cargoes of steel, lumber and housekeeping supplies.

The first completed structure was the Long Key Viaduct which had been delayed by the 1906 hurricane. One hundred and eighty-six 35-foot reinforced concrete arches extended over 2.15 miles of water required 286,000 barrels of cement, 177,000 cubic yards of crushed rock, 106,000 cubic yards of sand, 612,000 feet of piling, 5,700 tons of reinforcing rods and 2,600,000 feet of dressed timber. A photo of an actual train crossing Long Key Viaduct soon became the trademark of the Key West Extension.

By January 22, 1908, the Overseas Railroad was half finished with one hundred and six miles completed. William J. Krome, assistant to Meredith, brought his bride down to live in a Marathon cottage. The location was also headquarters for engineers, recreational facilities, barracks for workers, a hospital, shops, power plant and recreational facilities.

Regular passenger service began in February, 1908 with stations at Long Key, Grassy Key, Key Vaca and Knights Key Dock. A long trestle at Knights Key carried trains to a large dock where steamships of the Peninsula & Occidental S.S. Company (owned by Flagler) carried passengers and freight between Knights Key and Havana, 115 miles away. Infrastructure included a railway station and ferry terminal, customs office, post office and a ferry to accommodate overnight passengers.

On January 4, 1909, the first through passenger train between New York and Knights Key began regular service (called the New York and Florida Special) and carried Pullman sleeping cars on a daily schedule. A reporter for the *Key West Citizen* wrote: "Key West looks northward to the fast approaching bands of steel which will bind her to the mainland and dreams of the not too far distant day when she shall be a large and bustling and important city, the metropolis of Southern Seas."

Long Key, with its sandy beaches, was planted with coconut palm trees. Flagler built a half-mile of narrow gauge railroad to pick up guests at dockside who were seated on straw cushions and taken (by way of a tunnel beneath the Overseas RR line) to the Atlantic Ocean side where cottages were available. Author-sportsman Zane Grey came via rail while some wealthy visitors came by boat, docking their yachts on the Gulf side of Long Key. In 1907, railroad enthusiasts were convinced that since the Long Key

Viaduct had been built successfully, why not a nine-mile railroad bridge across the Gulf of Mexico and all the islands to Key West?

Krome was afraid that 79 year-old Flagler would not live long enough to see the Extension finished. He decided to work through the hurricane season in order to speed the completion of the railroad. He wrote:

> "No man has ever passed through one of the West India hurricanes and boasted that he had no fear of it. Indeed, lack of fear is dangerous. The responsibility resting upon the engineers for the safety of the men and for the preservation of equipment is heavy. There is no harbor along the entire line of the grade that is safe from hurricane damage. We must be ready for it when it comes; we must have the workmen well in hand to prevent panic. We must have done all we could to save our machinery and camp outfit. We have found it more economical to sink our floating equipment in the most protected waters and raise it and repair it when the storm has passed."

The great loss of life in the 1906 hurricane caused FEC officials to take extra precautions: telephone wires were strung from Miami to report weather information faster; no women were allowed to live in camp homes later than August; transportation was provided for all the most necessary personnel.

In early 1909, project manager J.C. Meredith was taken ill and passed away on April 20, 1909. The slightly-built Meredith was a diabetic, a condition that he kept to himself. Meredith was buried in a Miami cemetery where his gravestone was decorated with a bronze plaque with wording approved by Flagler:

> "In memory of Joseph Carroll Meredith, Chief Engineer in the construction of the Key West Extension of the Florida East Coast Railway, who died at his post of duty, April 20, 1909. This memorial is erected by the railway company in appreciation of his skill, fidelity, and devotion in this last and greatest work of his life."

Flagler then appointed William J. Krome as the new project manager. The thirty-two year old Krome, a graduate of the University of Illinois and Cornell and a member of the Society of American Engineers, faced a daunting task. The project at hand was the building of a bridge more than 35,000 feet long, nearly four times the length of the Long Key Viaduct. One of his first decisions was whether to continue work on the bridge through the upcoming 1909 hurricane season.

Krome finally made his decision to continue construction despite the risks, through the summer and fall of 1909.

The 1909 hurricane struck in September with unrivaled ferocity. The concrete viaducts withstood the storm with its winds of 125 miles per hour. But, more than 40 miles of embankment and track washed out in the Upper Keys. Boulders weighing from 6 to 10 tons were rolled like pebbles into the sea. It cost extra millions of dollars and two additional years to repair the damage.

Following the warnings of the Conch island people that there were not enough bridges for the free flow of water, Krome now put in eighteen miles of bridges where the original plans had called for six.

Flagler was undeterred. In a letter to James Ingraham he admitted that the company's losses had been formidable, "but to the general public we must all keep a stiff upper lip and admit nothing." To other associates, he urged, "My recommendation is to hoist Key West's flag high, keep it waving and let it bear the inscription, "Nil Desperandum"".

By November 8th, less than a month after the storm had supposedly wiped out the line, the company had managed to restore passenger service to Knight's Key, with construction and supply trains following in the wake.

Engineers were concerned about the effects of salt spray upon the steel deck spans and reinforcing gardens. An FEC paint laboratory discovered that no paint could be formulated to provide protection against the local effects of salt spray for more than two years. Consequently, painting crews would be required to work year-round to prevent deterioration by rusting. The investigation of the effect of wave and salt action on the concrete support piers provided a more optimistic conclusion. The results of submerged concrete samples revealed that while the concrete might erode slightly up to one-sixteenth of an inch, the deterioration would eventually stop with the formation of algae and other marine-aided deposits which would seal the concrete.

The finished bridge required 13 spans of 128 feet long, 13 spans of 186 feet long and 9 arches of 80 feet long. The arches were dovetailed at the joints with space for contraction and expansion. Arched steel trusses were placed on top of these spans to support the railroad tracks from above.

The island of Big Pine Key offered a strange difference from the rest of the Keys. Some agriculturists thought that it was a left-over part of the Appalachian ridge on the mainland. It was heavily wooded with pine trees and had fresh water close to the surface, a rarity compared to other Keys. It was always subject to forest fires during hurricanes. But Big Pine provided buttonwood for fuel for the charcoal kiln makers.

In September 1910, another hurricane hit the Lower Keys and lasted thirty hours. Below Marathon, the roadbeds in Bahia Honda, Spanish Harbor, Big Pine and Ramrod Keys became sea-filled channels. The worst blow, however, was the discovery that the combined strength of the water and wind had displaced the foundation of the center span of the Bahia Honda Bridge, the one span that had required a full shipload of concrete to anchor.

But Krome had no time to brood over hurricane damage. His target year for completion of the Key West Extension was 1913. The chief constructing engineer wrote, "It was near the end of February 1911, when we were asked, 'Can you finish the road down to Key West so we can put Mr. Flagler there in his private car over his own rails out of Jacksonville on his next birthday, January 2nd. I did some close figuring and finally replied that we could complete the road by January 22 of that year should no storm overtake us, or no unforeseen delay set us back." Krome was able to keep his promise with twenty-four hours to spare.

This commitment required cutting a year off the schedule. In order to accomplish this speed-up, dredging, filling and concrete pouring continued without stop in order to complete the final link of the remaining 50 miles. In addition to completing the trackage, General Manager Parrott was given the task of building the railroad terminal and shipping docks on Key West. The town has been in existence since 1820. During its first years it was a haven for pirates who used the Caribbean as their private hunting ground until 1822 when the U.S. Government asked Commodore David Porter to get rid of them. At the time, Key West was lined with coral reefs on the Atlantic side which were mostly unmarked until the late 1800s. When ships went aground during storms, Key Westers saved lives of passengers and crewmen. Then they salvaged the cargoes by reaping a large share of the profits for themselves. It is said that nearly every home in Key West was furnished with the salvage from sunken ships: rugs, dishware, silver, china, satins, linens and brocades. In fact, some shipwrecked passengers settled permanently in Key West to enjoy the mostly wonderful climate and local hospitality.

With the construction of lighthouses, fewer and fewer ships were wrecked on its shores. In 1880, Key West became the cigar capital of the world when thousands of Cubans settled there to avoid Spanish tyranny and ultimately produced one hundred million cigars a year. In addition, fine sheepswool sponge found in local waters, a turtle industry and fishing became lucrative businesses.

Incredibly, by 1890, Key West became the most populous city in all Florida. When General Manager Parrott reported that there was not enough dry land in Key West for the Overseas Railroad terminal, Flagler responded, "Then make some." Parrott hired Howard Trumbo to supervise the completion of the terminal project. His crew constructed a bulkhead extending in a broad arc around the northwest side of the island where the water was shallow. Thousands of cubic feet of mud and marl were pumped up from the bottom of the Gulf to provide a foundation for rail yards, terminal buildings and docks. So vast was the project that

U.S. Navy officials in Key West protested claiming that Parrott was digging up half the bay with fill that might be needed for defense purposes someday. Parrott replied that if a time came when the Navy needed its mud, he would be return it from whence it came. Trumbo's work proceeded and by January 1912 the terminal facility at Man-of-War Harbor was completed including a permanent pier 1,700 feet long by 134 feet wide where steamships could dock. Arriving passengers were able to walk a few steps across a platform and board a ship bound for Havana. Five to six hundred freight cars could be stored on the sidings ready to load cargo brought from the Caribbean, Central and South America to provide pineapples, tropical fruit and vegetables all winter.

The *Florida Times Union* wrote, "The Old Key West- one of the most unique of the world's little cities- is shaking off its lethargy… the spirit of progress and development will be greater than ever."

On January 21, 1912, a bridge manager closed the crossover span at the Knights Key trestle, allowing trains to go all the way to Key West. A pilot train with only a small crew left Knights Key and found the new trackage in prime condition. This was the first train to enter Key West after almost seven years of construction of the Key West Extension. The process of rail building that had begun in 1892 was complete. There were now 366 miles of track connecting Jacksonville with Miami and 156 more linking Miami with Key West.

That same morning, the Extension Special left Miami to carry eighty-two year-old Henry Morrison Flagler from his home, Whitehall in Palm Beach. The engine and its tender were followed by five passenger cars filled with notable people and FEC officials. The last car was Flagler's private Car 91 built to his specifications in 1886 at the Jackson & Sharp plant in Wilmington, Delaware. On that notable morning, Flagler was frail and his sight was failing but nothing was going to stop him. Not after spending $12 million on a series of hotels, $18 million on his land-based railroad and $20 million or more on his "last train to Paradise." Flagler boarded his private railroad car in Palm Beach for the 220-mile trip that culminated in Key West to fulfill his dream. Custom-made Car 91 was a copper-roofed pleasure palace of a railroad car, containing a Victorian-styled wood-paneled lounge, sleeping berths for visitors, and a private stateroom with bath for Flagler. It also contained a copper-lined shower, a dining table and a small food preparation area with an icebox and a wood stove.

Among the guests on board on that historic morning was Assistant Secretary of War Robert Shaw Oliver, the personal representative of President William Howard Taft. A reporter for the *Key West Florida Sun* wrote "The railroad magnate has extended his rod, and the sea has been divided."

In his book *"Key West: The Old and The New"*, Jefferson Browne wrote:

> "Henry M. Flagler's railroad…. is man's last word on that marvelous style of construction and will echo through the ages to come. Everything that went into the construction of this work obeyed his will…. The Greeks before Troy suffered no greater hardships, no greater heroism."

When Henry Flagler stepped out of Car 91, onto the observation platform in Key West he heard an ovation that he had never before encountered. He had "ridden his own iron" to Key West at last. He was welcomed by the mayor of Key West who presented him with a gold and silver commemorative plaque bearing his likeness. Another golden tablet came from the men who built the railroad over seven long years and was presented to "Uncle Henry".

After a children's chorus of one thousand voices sang popular songs and a military band played patriotic marches, Flagler was able to speak: "We have been trying to anchor Key West to the mainland and anchor it we have done. I thank God that from the summit I can look back over the twenty-five or twenty-six years since I became interested in Florida with intense satisfaction at the results that have followed."

After suffering through three devastating hurricanes (1906, 1909 and 1910) and the loss of some 700 lives, the railroad track finally reached Key West. Representatives from France, Great Britain, Italy and Brazil attended the completion ceremonies. The *Miami Herald* of January 22, 1912 reported,

> "The city is flooded with people; it is bedecked with bunting and colors. Its splendid harbor is floating war vessels of many nations and its people are overjoyed and enthusiastic over the coming of the railroad, the realization of their dreams of years. Their hearts are open to the world. They are going to do themselves proud."

Construction took seven years from 1905-1912. Six thousand men worked on the railroad from all parts of the world. According to E.H. Sheeran, general superintendent, a large percentage came from New York City's "Skid Row." Besides handling thousands of tons of steel and concrete, they also dug 20 million cubic yards of rock, sand and marlstone (a calcium carbonate lime rich mudstone which contains clay and silt). All this difficult work was done mostly without the benefit of modern machinery or horsepower of any kind.

The celebration in Key West lasted for days. The official souvenir program written by FEC's George M. Chapin included five nights of fireworks, boat tours of the railroad yards, yacht races and a fleet of U.S. Navy warships. A circus from Cuba performed nightly as did a Spanish opera company. Florida's governor Albert Gilchrist issued a proclamation: "The building of this great overseas railroad is of nationwide importance, second in importance only to the construction of the Panama Canal." President William Howard Taft sent a personal note of congratulations. After returning to the Whitehall Mansion in Palm Beach, Flagler wrote a letter to Joseph Parrott:

> *"The last few days have been full of happiness for me, made so by the expression of appreciation of the people for the work I have done in Florida. A large part of this happiness is due to the gift of the employees of the Florida East Coast Railway…. I beg you will express to them my most sincere thanks. I greatly regret that I cannot do it to each one in person.*
>
> *The work I have been doing for many years has been largely prompted by a desire to help my fellowmen, and I hope you will let every employee of the Company know that I thank him for the gift, the spirit that prompted it, and for the sentiment therein expressed."*

Soon after the FEC Extension Railroad arrived in Key West, regular ferry service to Havana was instituted. A Havana newspaper reported "This train, carrying the latest design all-steel Pullman drawing room and Standard sleeping cars, is electrically lighted and equipped with electric fans throughout. There is no change of cars between Key West and the Pennsylvania Station in the very heart of New York City." The train schedule reported that passengers could leave Havana at 10:30 AM daily, except Sundays, and arrive in New York two days later at 7:55PM. The Key West-Miami run required only four and one-half hours according to the printed timetable but often took six to seven hours.

But, as most passengers understood, delays on the new railroad lines were to be expected. One writer described passengers who could "watch the stately procession of southbound ocean steamers which pass in the great tide of traffic to the West Indies and to Central American and South American ports. Nor is it at all fanciful to suppose that if he is wise enough to carry along a fishing line and bait, he may find sport from the car platform should the train happen to halt on the Long Key or Bahia Honda viaduct."

For those guests who had utilized the Flagler resort hotels in St. Augustine, Ormond Beach, Daytona Beach, Palm Beach and Miami, a trip on the Overseas Railroad with a stop in Long Key was exciting. If the trip continued to Key West and included a boat trip to Havana, the traveler was overwhelmed with excitement. In fact, the Havana Special operated as an express all the way from New York to Miami but as a local with as many as forty-three stops on the way to Key West.

In 1912, when the Extension was opened, there were no ferries, only passenger steamers. Flagler had planned to build twelve piers at Key West, each 800 feet long and 200 feet wide. Each pier was to be covered by sheds with basins 200 feet in width, each basin providing berths for four large ships. Ferries were intended to carry Pullman cars from the Overseas Railroad so that passengers from New York need never leave their cars until they arrived in Havana. However, only three large steel ferries were built to carry freight cars:

- The *Henry M. Flagler* launched in 1915 was the largest car ferry in the world. It was 360 feet long with a 57-foot beam and was fitted with four standard-gauge tracks to hold thirty to thirty-five loaded freight cars
- Two similar ferries the *Joseph R. Parrott* and the *Estrada Palma* started service soon thereafter.

By 1924, thirty-five hundred carloads of pineapples were handled through Key West annually. The Overseas Railroad had a reverse effect on Key West's population. It turned out that more people were leaving Key West than were arriving to stay. Many islanders hopped passenger trains for a better life on the mainland and never returned especially when the Great Depression of the 30s began to hurt Key West's economy. And before that in the 1920s, Prohibition became the law of the land with the ratification of the Eighteenth Amendment. Key West was never shut down during the dry years because Cuba as a source of liquor supply was so near. Furthermore, the islanders knowledge of secret places in the channels of the Keys allowed them to be successful rumrunners.

Despite Prohibition and the Depression the Key West Extension performed well from 1912 to 1935. The railroad employed divers to fulfill the safety regulations set by the Federal Government to check underwater concrete foundations of all bridges every two years. Maintenance men walked the 156-mile road from Miami to Key West inspecting each tie, each bolt, each rail. Because of this rigid safety routine, wrecks were scarce and when they occurred were due to human error.

In 1909, Henry Flagler was interviewed by Edwin LeFevre, one of the foremost financial writers in the United States. His reports were widely-reported and widely-respected.

Edwin LeFevre was trained as a mining engineer but became a journalist at age nineteen. He produced eight books during his fifty-three year writing career. He was a celebrated financial author made most famous by the publication of his *Reminiscences of a Stock Operator* which is considered a classic of American business writing.

LeFevre, 39 years-old at the time of his visit to Whitehall, was considered the leading Wall Street analyst. His article appeared in *Everybody's Magazine*. Before interviewing Flagler, LeFevre inspected the Flagler hotels and railroads and spoke to Flagler's key assistants. When he completed this research, he interviewed Flagler at the Whitehall mansion. LeFevre wrote,

> "I saw an old man with a high forehead rising in straight lines from the temples. His hair is of a clean, glistening silver, like the cropped mustache and the eyebrows. They set off his complexion, which is neither ruddy nor baby-pink, but what one might call a virile red. He has a straight nose and a strong chin. The head is well shaped. The eyes are a clear blue – some might say violet. They must have been very keen once; today their expression is not easy to describe – not exactly shrewd nor compelling nor suspicious; though you feel they might have been all of these, years ago. Withal, you are certain that

it is not age which has mellowed them; the change is more subtle; it is from within – eyes that gleam but never flame…. A handsome old man! Under his fourscore years his shoulders have bowed slightly, but there is no semblance of decay.

You see in his face good concentration; good observation, without undue alertness; meditation without self-abstraction; attentiveness without tension; indomitable will without stubbornness; a steady-gaited man, deliberate not from age nor from indifference, but from temperament and life habit."

LeFevre described St. Augustine and the Flagler hotels:

"You stop in St. Augustine to rest before proceeding south. It is an old town, St. Augustine: "The oldest city in the United States," they are careful to tell you. Also they point out a dozen "oldest" houses, none particularly interesting, and the old Spanish fort and the old slave market – which probably wasn't a slave market at all. In point of fact, the spirit of the place does not bear down very heavily on you with the antiquity…. Nevertheless, something here is different; I think it is because everywhere you see palms.

And utilizing to the utmost this palm motif are the Flagler hotels. They fit, these beautiful edifices, Spanish in architecture and gorgeously successful in the utter un-Americanness of their environment and general effect. Barely twenty years old, they look as if they had always been there, in that precise spot. They "belong", very decidedly…."

LeFevre traveled to Ormond Beach which he called "the most wonderful speedway in the world; that smooth (sand), just hard enough, and swept clean every day by the mighty broom of the tide." And then he described the Flagler hotel:

> "The Ormond Hotel is between the beach and the Halifax River. It is comfortable, and more homelike, than any other Flagler hotel, and the grounds have a more exotic look than in St. Augustine. You drive to Daytona along beautiful roads,
>
> past orange groves and the cottages of the winter residents, through streets bordered by trees heavily hung with Spanish moss. Beautiful places, Daytona and Ormond, with river and ocean "views"; but you must push southward to Palm Beach."

S.A.83—Hotel Ponce De Leon, St. Augustine, Fla.

SA-H724

Bird's Eye View of Alcazar and Cordova Hotels
from the Ponce de Leon, St. Augustine, Fla.
Noted for their Spanish and Moorish Architecture.

The Alcazar Court looking through King St., St. Augustine, Fla.

Moonlight on the Halifax

The Ormond Hotel, ORMOND, Fla.

At the Races, DAYTONA, Fla.

The Royal Poinciana Hotel & Grounds, PALM BEACH, Florida.   3154.

The "Breakers" from the Golf Links,
Palm Beach, Fla.

Casino Pool at The Breakers Hotel, Palm Beach, Fla.—76

526. HOTEL ROYAL PALM AND BISCAYNE BAY, MIAMI, FLA.

Florida East Coast Railway, Key West Extension, Express Train crossing Famous Long Key Viaduct, Florida.

Off to Sea with No Seasickness Over the New Overseas Highway on the Way to Key West, Florida

13438 "WHITEHALL" HOME OF THE LATE MR. H. M. FLAGLER, PALM BEACH, FLA.

Whitehall Hotel, Palm Beach, Florida   12

LeFevre was astounded by Palm Beach and the Royal Poinciana Hotel:

> "It is the heart of our Riviera. The train stops at the very gates of the Royal Poinciana – the largest wooden building in the world used exclusively for hotel purposes. You notice long, colonnaded porches and no architectural pretensions – a hotel that has grown by means of additions as it grew in popularity.
>
> If the Royal Poinciana Hotel neither awes you by its size nor charms you by its architecture, the grounds completely delight you. To make a lawn here was more difficult than it would have been to spread a sheet of solid silver on this spot, or on the golf links, where Mr. Flagler's engineers dumped thousands of carloads of earth. Lawns you have seen before; but not these curious trees and strange shrubs with poly- chromatic leaves; uncanny screw pines with clumps of exposed roots like writhing serpents upholding the trunk; the gaudy crimson blossoms of the hibiscus that suggest the red lights on a Christmas tree; palms of divers kinds, borders of century plants grown to huge size...."

LeFevre expressed the prejudicial word "Ethiopian" to describe African Americans who pulled the wheel chairs:

> "In an Ethiopian propelled wheel chair you go forth to see Palm Beach; no horses are allowed here. The hotel is on Lake Worth, and you take the drive along the shore. Bluebill ducks swim about and

dive with an air of doing it for your benefit. You see the garfish poking their noses into everything; the oldest of extant fishes, unchanged and "unevoluted" these hundred thousand years, they now help to intensify the feeling of being in a strange world….

On both sides of the Lake Drive grow coconut palms, graceful, lithe, almost animate. You see them gazing at themselves in the mirror of the lake, perennially fascinated by their beauty. Along the glaring white road, through tennels of verdure, the noiseless wheel chair carries you, each strange tree adding impressions of a land utterly foreign.

You return and drive through palm bordered streets to the "Jungle Trail" – a man-made labyrinthine road, cut tunnel-like through banks of vegetation; past weird, misshapen trees… on out to the "Breakers," the other Flagler hotel, and the pier…. The ocean is very blue, save near the horizon, where it is green. There is the smell of the sea and the roar of the sea – that and the sky and its eternal azure challenge to the water."

LeFevre pushed on to Miami which was formerly the southernmost Flagler development. He described it as a business town whose major product was fruit. He wrote, "where nothing was, a few years ago, you see streets, brick buildings, hotels, banks, churches, schools, cottages not of "resorters" but of residents…. The Royal Palm – the local Flagler hotel – strikes you as the only "resort" feature here."

He then described the concrete viaduct which was Flagler's railroad:

"When I was down there a year ago, the late J.C. Meredith, construction engineer, had his headquarters at Knight's Key. In and out of the construction camps he flitted in his launch, his binoculars to his eyes, like a general observing the movements of his troops on the battlefield. You could see telephone poles sticking out of the water in the shallow places, for all the world like lines of skirmishers and scouts. On the deck of his launch, inspecting the work, he explained remarkable achievements in a remarkably matter-of-fact way. Then he spoke about himself:

"It was very strange, at first, for me to work for Mr. Flagler, on account of his point of view. With him it is never a case of *How much will it cost*? Nor of *Will it pay*? – which are the inevitable and perfectly proper questions for corporations to ask of their engineers...

I was told to make my studies and my estimates. We had lots of problems to solve, and I was quite a long time at it, and I knew how he desired to see the work rushed, but I never heard a word from him; not one request for haste. When the report was ready, Mr. Parrott and I took it to Mr. Flagler. He heard how we proposed to do it. We stopped before we came to the estimates of cost. And Mr. Flagler stood up and looked at us and said: '*Well, let's get to work*!' It was the most serious work he had planned to do in Florida. Perhaps he felt the occasion called for some comment, for he looked at me and said very quietly: 'I want to see it done before I die.' That is all he said."

The engineer was an unemotional, deliberate man of the von Moltke type. He paused and looked at me. Then he said, very earnestly, *"Mr. LeFevre, there isn't one of us who wouldn't give a year of his life to have Mr. Flagler see the work completed!"*

LeFevre summarized Flagler's incredible accomplishments:

"It is to be doubted whether mere figures can give an adequate idea of the magnitude of Flagler's work, He has spent $41,000,000 in Florida; that is, his investment in incorporated enterprise amounts to that, divided roughly as follows: $18,000,000 in the old railroads, including the development of towns, $10,000,000 in the Key West Extension, $12,000,000 in hotels, and $1,000,000 in steamboat and outside enterprises. This sum does not include his charities, churches and divers donations, for neither he nor any one else has kept the figures. The value of the taxable property in the counties exclusively reached by the Flagler roads has increased over fifty millions since he began. And there are today only about 25,000 acres under cultivation for fruit and vegetables out of a total of about 3,500,000 acres now available or such cultivation. Flagler has made the East Coast of Florida.

LeFevre recapped the construction of Flagler's hotels:

"The construction of the Ponce de Leon Hotel began in 1885. The house opened in December 1888. The Alcazar was completed shortly after. The Ormond Hotel was purchased in 1890, and enlarged from time to time. The Royal Poinciana at Palm Beach, originally a five-hundred-room house, was opened in February 1894; it now has 2,000 rooms. The Breakers was completed in 1895, destroyed by fire in 1903, and entirely rebuilt on the old site. It is a four-hundred-room house. The Royal Palm at Miami was completed and opened for the season of 1896-97. At Nassau, the Colonial, a four-hundred-room house, was opened in 1899. Flagler purchased other property there, including the Hotel Victoria, from the English Government. The Continental, at Atlantic Beach, Florida, a two-hundred-room summer hotel, opened in May 1901. His railroad carried one million passengers in 1908.

Steamship service was first inaugurated to Nassau in 1895 by the Florida East Coast Steamship Company, owned by Flagler. In 1896 the Key West line was opened, and, in the winter of that year, the operation was extended to the Havana line. There is now a daily service. In 1902, the Florida East Coast Steamship Company was consolidated with the Plant Steamship Company. Flagler owns one-half of the stock of the consolidation."

LeFevre found Flagler unique among capitalists. It was not money which spurred him but building and creation.

I do not know whether I have succeeded in making clear what I mean by saying that in Florida Henry M. Flagler found his Second Youth and was able to do a work that only youth ever does. It is an amazing work, even in this land of rapid development. Where others have helped, he has formed growth. That it is a work of vast importance is obvious. That it is unique is due to the impossibility of finding a man of Flagler's mind and Flagler's wealth and Flagler's business experience, having the attitude of Flagler toward his fellow-men. To my mind his most remarkable exploit was the changing of his own point of view, of his attitude toward his fellow-men, so completely, at so advanced an age. You must admit that he has done as a man in his prime does. It is easy to give; it is not easy to give as Flagler has given – money and service. And if the magnitude of his accomplishment grows the more you ponder it, so does the man's character appear more remarkable the more you reflect. It is therefore not so difficult, after all, to visualize the man as he is today, at eighty years, *in the flower of his Second Youth.*"

LeFevre found Flagler to be unknowable. He found him to be modest, wise and unassuming. A man who with his unique energies provided life opportunities for thousands, ultimately millions of people. Yet, finally a man who kept a only secret, who, despite all his virtues, had in his seventy-ninth year, by choice, one friend in the world – Dr. Andrew Anderson in St. Augustine, Florida.

There are, however, other rewards on earth than friendship, and Flagler was about to enjoy one of them, called glory.

Flagler continued to work at the Whitehall Mansion in Palm Beach or at Satan's Toe, near Mamaroneck, NY on the Long Island Sound from which he commuted regularly to his Manhattan office. When Henry and Mary Lily weren't in Mamaroneck, they would likely be at the Hotel Mount Washington in Bretton Woods, New Hampshire. This spectacular resort hotel was designed by the architect Charles Alling Gifford who was recommended to the owner Joseph Stickney by Henry Flagler. The hotel had a railroad station and coaches to bring guests to the hotel, it had a golf course designed by Donald Ross, it had an artificial lake, bridle paths, wagon roads, telegraph, running water, private bathrooms, an elevator, modern refrigerator equipment, its own electric power plant, a facility for making illuminating gas should the electricity fail, a one-of-a-kind press to print the daily menus and a daily newspaper for the guests. It had a large barn for horses and a garage for automobiles along with quarters for chauffeurs, dormitories for the staff, an orchestra, a choir, a heated indoor swimming pool and a billiard parlor. A doctor and two nurses were on duty on the premises.

Normally, to avoid the mosquito season of Palm Beach the Flaglers would stay till the end of February, then move by train to the cooler St. Augustine until mid-May. Then, they usually went by train or yacht to Mamaroneck. But, in the winter of 1913, Henry and Mary Lily prolonged their stay at the Whitehall Mansion. On March 15, 1913, Henry fell down a short flight of stairs in the large downstairs bathroom. Because Mary Lily and a few servants were the only people in the large mansion, it was several hours before he was found. Flagler was transferred to a beach cottage where he was treated by his own doctor, Owen Keenan and Dr. Newton Shaffer, an orthopedic surgeon from New York. Mary Lily telegraphed Harry Harkness Flagler, his estranged son who hadn't seen his father since his own wedding in 1894. He had never been to Whitehall. He had never met Mary Lily.

After an estrangement of nearly 20 years, Harry was determined to do something for his father and reported, "He had been moved to a cottage on the ocean front belonging to the hotel. This was because of the extreme heat. When I heard of his worsening condition, I telegraphed offering to go to him if he wanted me. I was not allowed to do so while there was a chance of his recognizing me. He was kept constantly under drugs and was practically in a coma the three or four days after my arrival until his death." At no time did Flagler appear to recognize his only son and his only surviving child. Flagler died on May 20, 1913 at 10 AM. He was buried in St. Augustine in a dedicated mausoleum next to his first wife, Mary Harkness Flagler and their daughter, Jennie Louise Flagler Benedict and Jennie's baby.

During its twenty-three years of operation, no passenger or freight train plunged off any of the Overseas bridges into the ocean. From 1912 to 1935, the Key West Extension performed creditably and was called the "Eighth Wonder of the World." It took the Great Depression followed by the Great Hurricane on September 2, 1935 to end its operation. Up to that fatal day, half-a-million passengers made successful trips over the 156-mile road. Its route transversed twenty-nine islands connected by sturdy bridges and embankments. Travelers watched dolphins leaping from deep channels and sharks racing the train as it traveled slowly across great bridges. A trip on the Overseas Railroad had the excitement of an ocean voyage without the risk of seasickness.

Serious hurricanes, which delayed the completion of the Key West Extension during its construction, did not strike the railroad for twenty-five years. A monster storm in 1926 hit Miami hard and destroyed the new city of Coral Gables. Other hurricanes damaged parts of South Florida but skipped Flagler's Overseas Railroad. That is, until the Labor Day weekend of 1935. On Sunday, September 1, 1935, as the storm approached Andras Island in the Bahamas, less than one hundred miles from the U.S. mainland, it was packing winds of seventy-five miles per hour. It was predicted that the storm would pass through the channel separating Cuba from the Keys. But less than forty hours later, the storm veered northward toward the Keys and became a Category 5 storm with winds of two hundred miles per hour and, to this day, one of the strongest ever to hit the United States.

Up until then, the Galveston, Texas Hurricane of 1900 was the deadliest in recorded history which caused 6,000 deaths. Next was this 1935 hurricane with winds estimated at more than two hundred miles per hour. For the men working on the Overseas Highway, the damage was severe and the reported death toll was thought to be far too low owing to an uncertain Keys census and a general laxity in record-keeping by the Federal Emergency Relief Administration. (FERA).

For the men working on the Overseas Railroad, the record-keeping was inaccurate. The "vets" as the highway workers were called by the locals, were largely World War I veterans who had marched on Washington a few years earlier demanding payment of the veteran's bonus promised by Congress but never paid. President Hoover and General Douglas MacArthur dispersed the "bonus army" with armed troops and tear gas at Anacostia Flats in Washington, D.C. President Franklin Roosevelt developed a more humane response when government agencies provided the veterans with employment in the Keys. Unfortunately, these men were not being supervised by seasoned FEC project engineers. The camps that had been built were not the strong reinforced FEC shelters but primarily flimsy temporary structures and tents. Furthermore, the Weather Bureau downplayed the threat of the storm. The *Miami Herald* made no mention of the impending hurricane "Miami To Observe Labor Holiday" was its inadequate headline with "Program Includes Parade, Sports, Picnic and Addresses" as its misleading subhead. While the forecast was for showers later in the day, there was no mention of the impending hurricane.

But on September 2, 1935, the last train to leave Miami for the Keys was sucked into giant centrifuge of the killer hurricane. Along the Keys hundreds of highway workers awaited rescue. The great wave swept homes and barracks before it and toppled railroad cars as if they were plastic toys. Of the thousand or more persons in the area more than half perished. So ended the struggle against one of the most destructive forces of nature. During the twelve-year construction of the Overseas Railroad, Flagler and his engineers survived three severe hurricanes and managed to anchor Key West to the mainland with their single track railroad by 1916. Luckily Flagler did not live long enough to see his railroad destroyed. The Key West Extension never earned a profit. After the hurricane, Flagler's family and officials of the FEC decided not to rebuild the Overseas Railroad. They sold it for $640,000 to the state of Florida after it had been appraised by the federal government at $27,280,000 and which could have been repaired for $1,500,000.

Despite the crippling damage caused by the 1935 hurricane, all of the Overseas Railroad's great concrete viaducts were still standing.

They were the backbone of the two-lane automobile highway built by the state of Florida that is in use to this day. As early as 1928, the U.S. Congress had passed legislation creating an Overseas Highway across the Keys. Courageous motorists could actually drive from Miami to Key West by utilizing several ferry services. The highway conversion was completed in 1938 and provided a way for thousands of tourists to reach the milder tropical climate of Key West which became a thriving tourist destination.

After Henry Flagler's death, Mary Lily lived in her permanent suite at the Plaza Hotel in New York, at the Whitehall Mansion in Palm Beach and in Newport, Rhode Island at the Pembroke Jones home. In November 1916, she married an old beau, Robert Worth Bingham who was an attorney in Louisville, Kentucky. Unfortunately, Mary Lily passed away of an heart attack only eight months later. Bingham inherited $5 million and purchased daily newspapers which were merged into the *Louisville Courier-Journal*. The remainder of her $100 million estate was divided between her brother, sister and her niece, Louise Clisby Wise. Miss Wise also inherited Whitehall and Kirkside. After seven years, she sold Whitehall and and in 1926, the new owner added a ten-floor tower and converted it into the luxurious Whitehall Hotel. It operated as a hotel until 1959 when Flagler's granddaughter Mrs. Jean Flagler Matthews (1910-1979) purchased the property. She wrote:

> "….during my years of growing up, rarely was the name of Henry Morrison Flagler mentioned. I knew from my sister that there had been an estrangement between father and grandfather, but not until I rented a house in Miami Beach did I begin to know of grandfather's accomplishments. That was

in 1938-1939. In 1940, when I came to Palm Beach, many questions were asked, so I scurried around to the libraries in order to have some idea of his many accomplishments. The more I learned, the more I gazed at Whitehall and started the mind thinking about what should be done. One day, while mulling on the problem, I heard that a spa was going to open at Whitehall, and that the Marble Hall would be used for dressing room cubicles- that did it. The next morning I attended a board meeting.... And during the Treasurer's Report, leaned over to my then lawyer and said, "I want to acquire Whitehall as a memorial to grandfather." He looked at me as if I were crazy..... It all happened in the nick of time, as hammer and chisel were about to be lowered."

Whitehall opened as a museum with an appropriate Restoration Ball on February 6, 1960 after the tower was demolished.

The state of Florida used the railroad's viaducts, bridges and roadbed as the foundation of the overseas highway. In 1938, the last link was connected and U.S.1 was open at long last from Miami to Key West.

Flagler's system of hotels and railroads were managed by Joseph Parrott of Oxford, Maine who died only five months after Flagler. William Beardsley was elected president and had a successful management career. The Florida East Coast Railway consisted of 764 miles of track. The value of the properties rose from $5.5 million in 1894 to $15 million in 1914. Following Mary Lily's death, Will Kenan and his two sisters owned the Florida East Coast Railway until it went bankrupt during the Depression.

Despite the loss of the FEC, the Kenans did not go broke. Will Kenan died in 1965 with an estate worth $160 million. His two sisters died soon thereafter leaving estates of $160 million each.

Besides the Florida East Coast Hotel Company, the Florida East Coast Railway Company and the Model Land Company, the Flagler System also included the Miami Electric Light Company, the West Palm Beach Water Company, various smaller land companies and later the Florida East Coast Car Ferry Company. Flagler also owned controlling interests in various Florida newspapers including the *Miami Herald*, the *St. Augustine Record*, the *Miami News* and the *Jacksonville Times-Union*.

Henry Flagler's estranged son Harry Harkness Flagler graduated from Columbia University in 1897 at 26 years of age. He was one of the most important figures in the New York musical world and became president of the Symphony Society of New York and the Philharmonic-Symphony Society. When he died on July 1, 1952, at 81, the *New York Times* obituary wrote,

> "...although those who knew Mr. Flagler well found him possessed of evident business capacity, he never engaged in business and kept aloof from the affairs of the Standard Oil Company. Nor did he show interest in the large... holdings... of his father in Florida. His temperament was artistic and as early as 1903 he became secretary of the Permanent Fund Orchestra, which planned the development of the Philharmonic Society.
>
> Having reorganized the Symphony Society of New York and its orchestra, Mr. Flagler served as its president from 1914 to 1928 and made himself

responsible for its entire financial banking. After its merger with the Philharmonic Society, he became president of the new group and continued to see that money was provided to keep the organization alive and up to its high musical standard. During the depression years, he made possible the very existence of the New York Philharmonic Symphony Orchestra."

Flagler's longtime assistant, James Ingraham said that the last conversation he had with Flagler was about the railroad around Lake Okeechobee. Said Ingraham:

"The last time I saw him, stretched out on his bed of suffering at Palm Beach, before his death, I had just returned from a trip to Okeechobee… He asked me to tell him about it, and I showed him some pictures and he gave me his last words on this subject, which were: "I hope you will succeed. I am sorry I have not been there. I wish I could go. I hope to go, but I am afraid I will never see that great lake and that great country."

He then put his hand on mine and said: "When were you at Miami?" I said: "I was there yesterday and the day before, came up from there this evening." He said: "Well, what about it, what are they doing?" I told him some things that were going on, and I told him that it was truly a magic city.

He said: "No, it is not a magic city. It is a city of eternal youth. Those men and women there are like boys and girls. They have never been hurt and they know no fear."

Apparently, there was no eulogy from Flagler's old partner John D. Rockefeller who did not attend the funeral. In his biography *"Henry Flagler: The Astonishing Life and Times of the Visionary Robber Baron Who Founded Florida"*, David Leon Chandler wrote:

"Once the Key West rails were laid, he liked to ride the line below Miami, ride in the engineer's cab and pull the cord and whistle his way through the keys.

In the days of the steam locomotive, many an engineer had his own way of sounding his whistle, Folks living along the railroad could tell the name of the engineer the moment he came within hearing distance. Some could make it sound off like a steam calliope in a circus parade.

Regulations banned unnecessary locomotive whistling on the mainland. But all restrictions seemed to end once a train, especially a freight, passed south of Jewfish Draw. If there were rules, no one on the keys was mean enough to tell Henry Flagler to enforce them; so the boys often broke loose. When Uncle Henry asked the engineer to play "Long Caleb McGee" or "Old Dan Tucker," he played it. And when Henry was in the cab, he played it for himself. It was loud and strong yet sweet and he could hear it well.

They kept playing the songs for 20 years after Henry was dead. They played until the steam locomotives themselves were no more."

Development of the mangrove swamp known as Miami Beach was begun one year before Flagler's death by Carl Graham Fisher (1874-939). Fisher was one of America's large-scale land developers who envisioned entire new cities springing out of the ground. Before I recount Fisher's extraordinary projects such as Miami Beach, the Indianapolis Speedway, the Lincoln and Dixie Highways and Montauk, Long Island, I will tell the story of Henry Bradley Plant, the remarkable developer of Florida's Gulf Coast.

Henry Bradley Plant (1819-1899)

Like Henry Morrison Flagler, Henry B. Plant built hotels to encourage northerners to come to Florida on his railroad lines. His magnum opus was the 500-room, Moorish-style Tampa Bay Hotel, which opened in 1891. Immense by any standard, the $3 million property is one-quarter mile long and features a domed dining room, a music room, a solarium. Still standing, the building is no longer an operating hotel. It is now used by the University of Tampa and includes the Henry B. Plant Museum.

In 1819, the year of Henry Plant's birth, Florida's population was estimated at 12,000, less than half of what it had been when the first Europeans came ashore in 1513. At that time, the native Indian tribes (Apalachee, Calusa and Timucua) had close to 30,000 population. Unfortunately, these tribes were systematically decimated between 1492 and 1650 by white man's diseases, the slave trade, and European wars of conquest. The destruction of the aboriginal tribes attracted other Indians to the Florida hunting grounds from Georgia and Alabama. Members of the Creek nation established farms, grazing lands and hunting villages in the more remote interior regions of Florida during the early 1800s.

Meanwhile, Florida's population was also increased by the influx of runaway and fugitive slaves some of whom joined with or were taken into slavery by various newly-arrived Indian tribes.

In 1830, a group of Indian tribes called the Five Civilized Tribes: the Cherokee, Chicksaw, Choctaw, Muscogee and Seminole were living as autonomous nations in the American deep south. The process of cultural transformation as proposed by George Washington and Henry Knox was being implemented. But American settlers had been forcibly proposing that the federal government remove Indians from the Southeast. Finally, President Andrew Jackson gained Congressional approval of the Indian Removal Act of 1830 which authorized the U.S. government to arbitrarily remove Indian title to lands in the Southeast. By the end of 1840, tens of thousands of Cherokee and other tribes had been forcibly removed from their land east of the Mississippi River. The forced relocation death marches were called "A Trail of Tears and Deaths. The marchers were subject to extortion and violence along the route to Oklahoma. They were forced to set out during the hottest and coldest months of the year, killing many. Exposure to the elements, disease and starvation, harassment by local white frontiersman and insufficient rations killed up to one-third of the Choctaw and other nations on the march.

The military actions and subsequent treaties enacted by Presidents Andrew Jackson and Martin Van Buren which Tennessee Congressman Doug Crockett had unsuccessfully voted against, directly caused the expulsion or death of thousands of Indians then living in the southeastern United States.

Alexis de Tocqueville, the French philosopher, witnessed the Choctaw removals while in Memphis, Tennessee in 1831,

"In the whole scene there was an air of ruin and destruction, something which betrayed a final and irrevocable adieu; one couldn't watch without feeling one's heart wrung. The Indians were tranquil, but somber and taciturn. There was one who could speak English and of whom I asked why the Chactas were leaving their country. "To be free," he answered, could never get any other reason out of him. We… watch the expulsion… of one of the most celebrated and ancient American peoples."

Nearly 17,000 Choctaws made the move to what would be called Indian Territory and then later Oklahoma. About 2,500 to 6,000 died along the trail of tears. Approximately 6,000 Choctaws remained in Mississippi in 1831 after the initial removal efforts. The Choctaws who chose to remain in newly formed Mississippi were subject to legal conflict, harassment, and intimidation. The Choctaws "have had our habitations torn down and burned, our fences destroyed, cattle turned into our fields and we ourselves have been scourged, manacled, fettered and otherwise personally abused, until by such treatment some of our best men have died." The Choctaws in Mississippi were later reformed as the Mississippi Band of Choctaw Indians and the removed Choctaws became the Choctaw Nation of Oklahoma.

In the winter of 1838, the Cherokee began the 1,000-mile march with scant clothing and most on foot without shoes or moccasins. The march began in Red Clay, Tennessee, the location of the last Eastern capital of the Cherokee Nation. Because of the diseases, the Indians were not allowed to go into any towns or villages along the way; many times this meant traveling much father to go around them. After crossing Tennessee and Kentucky, they arrived at the Ohio Rive across from Golconda in southern Illinois about the 3rd of December 1838. Here the starving Indians were charged a dollar a head (equal to $22.22 today) to cross the river on "Berry's Ferry" which typically charged twelve cents, equal to $2.67 today. They were not allowed passage until the ferry had serviced all others wishing to cross and were forced to take shelter under "Mantle Rock," a shelter bluff on the Kentucky side, until "Berry had nothing better to do." Many died huddled together at Mantle Rock waiting to cross. Several Cherokee were murdered by locals. The Cherokee filed a lawsuit against the U.S Government through the courthouse in Vienna, suing the government for $35 a head (equal to $777.77 today) to bury the murdered Cherokee.

In 1987, about 2,200 miles of trails were authorized by federal law to mark the removal of 17 detachments of the Cherokee people. Called the "Trail of Tears National Historic Trail", it traverses portions of nine states and includes land and water routes.

In 1845, when Florida became a state, the remaining body of native Americans were forced to relocate to Arkansas except for those diehards who hid out in the Everglades. Those former Indian hunting lands in central Florida became cowboy-owned cattle kingdoms and large agricultural farms where cotton and fruit crops were planted and harvested by labor gangs of black slaves.

Henry Bradley Plant was born in Branford, Connecticut on December 27, 1819. His ancestors had lived in Connecticut since 1639. Plant's parents were Betsey and Anderson Plant, farmers of modest success. When Plant was only six years old, his father died. After several years, his mother remarried and Plant lived with them in Martinsburg, New York and later in New Haven, Connecticut. Plant was proud of his New England origins and maintained memberships in the Sons of the American Revolution and the New England Society all his life. He also kept a residence and office in New York City after 1875 and a summer home in Connecticut.

Plant's last bit of formal education ended in the eighth grade at the Lancastrian School in New Haven. At eighteen years of age, Plant declined his mother's offer to send him to Yale College and instead began his employment with the New Haven Steamboat Company as a "captain's boy". He worked hard to learn all aspects of the shipping business. He later worked for the Adams Express Company in various jobs in New York City and Augusta, Georgia. At age 23, Plant married Ellen Elizabeth Blackstone, daughter of a well-to-do state legislator, James Blackstone. The Plants had two sons, one of whom died at 18 months old. The second, Morton Freeman Plant, born in 1852, would later participate in his father's business. When Plant's wife developed congestion in her lungs, two physicians advised that she should go to a warner climate for a proper recovery. The Plants decided to leave New York on March 25, 1853 for a trip south by steamboat. When Plant and his wife arrived in Jacksonville, Florida, he noted that the city had inadequate wharf facilities and no vehicles to carry baggage or passengers to their hotel or local residence. After being warned about the condition of the hotels, Plant and his wife spent the first night in Florida in a private home and then traveled in a large dugout canoe paddled by a crew of black men to accommodations in a home at Strawberry Mills six miles distant on the St. Johns River. So poor was Mrs. Plant's recovery from the lung problem that she returned to Florida every winter during the remainder of her life and Henry did the same, spending thirty-nine winters in Florida. Over time, Mrs. Plant's health continued to decline and she died on February 28, 1861.

In Augusta, Georgia, the Plants lived in the following hotels: the Globe, Eagle, Phoenix and Planter's Hotel. When the oncoming Civil War was imminent, the Adams Express Company sold its southern business to Plant and his associates for $500,000. Plant signed five personal notes for $100,000 each. The company gained good will when it carried all clothing packages for Confederate soldiers free of charge. The Southern Express Company transported mail and packages as well as supplies, medicine, and payrolls for the Confederate States of America. By the end of the century, under Plant's continuous leadership, Southern Express employed 6,800 people in 15 states using 885 wagons and 1,450 horses. In addition, the business utilized 24,000 miles of railroad lines. The company ended independent operations when it was acquired by the American Railway Express Company in 1918.

Plant was instrumental in restoring economic health to the south during the Reconstruction era after the Civil War. Porter King, the Mayor of Atlanta, said in the *Atlantic Constitution*, "Georgia, the South and Atlanta owe more to Plant than to any other man."

While living in Augusta, an incident occurred which resulted in the purchase of a slave by Mr. Plant. A black slave by the name of Dennis Dorsey was rented by Plant to act as porter in his office. One summer when Plant was about to go north, Dennis said that his master was going to sell him for $1,500. Dennis said that "it is too much, I am not worth so much. You can buy me when you come back, as there is little danger of my being sold at that price." But Dennis was sold in Plant's absence. When Plant returned, he bought Dennis from a trader in Mobile, Alabama for $1,800 and brought him back to Augusta.

In 1873, twelve years after the death of his first wife, Henry Plant married Margaret Josephine Loughman daughter of Martin Loughman of New York City. Margaret, whose ancestry included nobility in Ireland, would later be a great help to Henry in the selection of furnishings for the Pullman palace cars, steamships and the Tampa Bay Hotel. The marriage was welcomed by the members of Plant's family and to show his appreciation, Henry took along his son Morton and mother on the honeymoon which included a tour of Europe. After the Civil War, Plant expanded his Southern Express Company by acquiring the Texas Express Co. and then was able to serve all the major cities in the south: Atlanta, Augusta, Charleston, Memphis, Montgomery, New Orleans and Savannah. Plant also became familiar with the railroad and hotel businesses.

Starting in 1879, Plant acquired the following railroads: Atlantic and Gulf, Savannah and Charleston and other short lines with partners, stockholders and other investors. In 1883, Plant and a dozen other investors, including Henry M. Flagler, acquired three-fifths of the South Florida Railroad which linked Savannah and Jacksonville with Tampa. These railroads carried passengers, timber, produce and river freight. Plant owned and operated steamboats on the St. Johns River. By the 1880s, the Plant Steamship Company was carrying passengers, freight and the United States mail between, Tampa, Key West and Havana.

The economic stimulant to railroad building in Florida was the Florida Internal Improvement Fund which in 1881 sold 4 million acres of land to Hamilton.

In the early part of 1882, Henry Plant came into contact with J. E. Ingraham, then president of a company that planned to build a railroad from Winter Park to Orlando to Tampa. Ingraham, who later became Flagler's chief lieutenant described his chance meeting with Plant:

> "About this time I was walking on Bay Street in Jacksonville with General Sanford when he

remarked to me, "Do you see the elderly gentleman on the other side of the street, the one wearing the long black broadcloth coat and silk hat? That is a man whom I think you ought to know. He is Henry B. Plant, president of the Savannah Florida and Western Railway Company, with whom I traveled on my last trip down from New York. After saying that I should like to meet Mr. Plant, I was introduced to him. He greeted me with "So you are the young man who is building a railroad from Sanford to somewhere in the south of Florida? Yes, Mr. Plant, I replied, we have a little narrow-gauge railroad down there and we feel quite proud of it. We expect to open that railroad to Kissimmee shortly, some time early next week, and I shall be more than glad to have you and your friends come down and be our guests at the opening. Mr. Plant told me of his purchase of a steamer, the Henry B. Plant, and his plan of running it, under command of Captain Jim Fitzgerald, to Sanford. Immediately I asked him for a connection for our road such as we had with the DeBarry line three days a week, saying I would like to have Mr. Plant's best connection for alternate days. He agreed to this request and also said he would join our party on the initial trip over the new road. Inquiring how many we could take care of, I told him to bring as many as he wished and that a special train would meet him and his party when the Henry B. Plant reached Sanford. Early on the appointed day…. we boarded a brand new train composed of a parlor car, coach and baggage car, the train crew having on new blue uniforms and white gloves…. The trip extended all the way to Belleair, then the terminus of the rail line, as St. Petersburg was at that time nothing more than a few cottages and huts occupied by fishermen. Mr. Plant was visibly impressed by the country along the route and, after returning from Belleair, he called a conference at which he asked, Mr. Ingraham, what can I do for you on this railroad project? "If you will give us connection with your St. John River steamer, and obtain for us through representation as to tickets and rates, I would be greatly obliged, I replied, continuing, that it was my ambition to extend our railroad to Tampa and to put on a line of steamers to Key West and Havana."

Then Plant asked "Do you think your stockholders would sell an interest in this property? "Ingraham replied "If you can see your way to purchasing, say, a three-fifths interest in the railroad extending it to Tampa and eventually putting on such a line of steamers, I am satisfied they would."

As a result of this conference, and a subsequent meeting in Boston, the Plant Investment Company became owner of a three-fifths interest in the South Florida Railroad, under contract to build the road from Kissimmee to Tampa. The work was pushed to completion very rapidly, and on the fourth day of January 1884, the South Florida Road was opened to Tampa. Governor Boxham and his entire cabinet, with their families, were among the guests of the company and were present at the driving of the last spike.

In 1885, Plant created the port of Tampa by building a causeway, a huge wharf and piers in deep water west of downtown Tampa at Port Tampa. The wharf accommodated steamships, trains, warehouses and a hotel known as the Inn at Port Tampa. The port ultimately had a capacity for berthing 26 ocean-going steamships, some of which provided steamship service to Key West, Cuba, other islands and Central America.

Most of Henry Plant's business interests were involved in the creation of railroad, steamboat and hotel services for the moving of people and goods for profit. Plant's mature water-based operations were widespread ranging from north-south steamboat service from Columbus, Georgia to Apalachicola, Florida for almost two decades and on the St. Johns River from Jacksonville to Palatka and Sanford using the "People's Line" name.

After Plant built the port, wharf and warehouse facilities at Tampa, he operated steamship lines on routes in the Gulf of Mexico from Mobile to Punta Gorda and Fort Myers. Plant also had extensive steamship service to Canada's maritime provinces. But the most important service was steamship service from Tampa to Havana, Cuba either via Key West or direct from Tampa. The "Federal Express/UPS" man of his time, Henry Plant owned and operated a huge organization that included several steamship lines, 14 railroad companies and eight hotels. It was estimated that Plant spent $3 million in creating Port Tampa.

At the end of the 19th century, the newly-created American leisure class began to travel extensively for pleasure. During this gilded age, Americans traveled on new and improved rail transportation made more comfortable with Fred Harvey's restaurants and resort hotels and George Pullman's Palace sleeping and dining cars.

The travelers of that era moved through Chicago on a slow journey westward on hard board seats in overcrowded crude coaches. Before

Fred Harvey, the stories of vile food and sloppy service were well-known. Dee Brown wrote in *Hear That Lonesome Whistle Blow* that one report said that "the chops were generally as tough as hanks of whipcord and the knives as blunt as a bricklayer's trowel" and the "chicken stew was really prairie dog." The lunchrooms were noisy and dirty, tables covered with stained cloths and served cracked dishes and bent flatware. Harvey's timing could not have been better when he started providing appetizing and affordable meals in clean and comfortable dining quarters.

In 1876, Fred Harvey opened his first railroad restaurant in Topeka, Kansas on the second floor of the little red Santa Fe depot. Good food, good cooking, spotless dining rooms, and courteous service, introduced by Fred Harvey in his first Harvey House, brought a booming business that pleased Santa Fe passengers and amazed Topeka residents.

The Santa Fe Railway provided the buildings for the Harvey restaurants where the passenger trains would stop twice daily for meals. The railroad carried all the produce and supplies needed by the Harvey restaurants including transporting the dirty linen to a central laundry facility. Fred Harvey hired, trained and supervised all personnel and provided for food and service. Harvey's policy was "maintenance of standards, regardless of cost." He believed that profits would grow if the food and service were excellent. "Meals by Fred Harvey" became the slogan of the Santa Fe Railway. Western hotels, before Harvey, were just shacks with cots. For guest who came from the East, those early facilities were intolerable.

From that modest beginning, the Harvey organization grew into a far-flung resort, restaurant, hotel and retail organization, with operations extending from Cleveland to the West Coast. During the 1880s and 1890s, Fred Harvey's unique restaurants and Harvey Houses opened, one after another, approximately every 100 miles along the Santa Fe through Kansas, Colorado, Texas, Oklahoma, New Mexico, Arizona and California. This was necessary, it was said, "To keep western traffic from settling in any one place where Fred Harvey served his incomparable meals."

In a formal contract with the railroad, signed in 1889, Harvey secured the right to operate all restaurants on the Sante Fe line west of the Missouri River. A subsequent 1893 contract gave him the rights to its dining-car service. He supplied the equipment, food, supplies, personnel and management and the railroad hauled them and the Harvey's employees for free. The profits were his to keep.

Harvey's food was the best quality, much of it supplied by local farmers. Just imagine the extraordinary planning and organizational efforts required to bring fruits and vegetables from California, beef from Texas, shellfish from the east coast and fresh water fish from the Great Lakes packed in ice to keep it fresh. Harvey owned and operated his own dairies to guarantee fresh milk and cheese. He brought in his own spring water so that Harvey-blended coffee would not be ruined by brackish local water. In the 1880s, Harvey customers were served full meals from oysters on the half shell to homemade pie, ice cream and coffee all along the Santa Fe route. Railroad buff and historian Lucius Beebe (1902-1966) wrote in the *American Heritage* magazine, "Harvey imposed a rule of culinary benevolence over a region larger than any Roman province and richer than any single British dominion save India."

In the late nineteenth century, three national expositions broke attendance records mainly because of the reliable new railroad service: the 1870 American Centennial Exhibition in Philadelphia, the 1893 World's Columbian Exposition in Chicago and the 1895 Cotton States and International Exposition in Atlanta. Encouraged and informed by new guidebooks, illustrated magazine articles and railroad advertising, travelers vacationed in American resorts from the east coast to the Rocky Mountains. Many of these resorts followed the railroads and were located in spectacular and picturesque locations: Bar Harbor, Maine; Newport, Rhode Island; New Jersey shore; White Mountains, New Hampshire; Berkshire Hills, Massachusetts; Adirondacks and Catskills Mountains, New York; Saratoga Springs and Ballston Spa, New York; Hot Springs, Arkansas; Lake Geneva, Wisconsin; Aiken, South Carolina; Hilton Head, South Carolina; Thomasville, Georgia; Rocky Mountains and Colorado Springs, Colorado.

The construction of new private lines was often followed by great new resort hotels. In Canada, American William Van Horne, president of the Canadian Pacific Railway, completed the construction of the CP Railroad across the continent. In order to attract passengers, Van Horne hired the famous New York architect Bruce Price to design two spectacular hotels: the Banff Springs Hotel opened in 1888 and the Chateau Frontenac in Quebec in 1893. Earlier, Price invented and patented the parlor bay-window cars for the CP Railroad, Pennsylvania Railroad and the Boston and Albany Railroad.

In Florida, in conjunction with his railroad construction, Henry B. Plant operated eight of the most successful resort hotels of the late 19th and early 20th century.

Henry Plant owned hotels in eight southwest Florida locations served by his railroad system. He developed and built three hotels: the Inn at Port Tampa (1888), the Tampa Bay Hotel (1891) and the Hotel Belleview (1897). He purchased and renovated the Hotel Kissimmee (1883), the Ocala House (1884), the Seminole Hotel (1886), the Hotel Punta Gorda (1887), and the Fort Myers Hotel (1897).

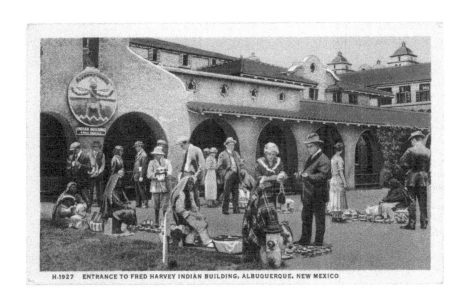

H-1927   ENTRANCE TO FRED HARVEY INDIAN BUILDING, ALBUQUERQUE, NEW MEXICO

Alvarado Hotel, Albuquerque, New Mexico.

One of the Beautiful New Club-Lounge Cars on the Santa Fe Scout

The Belleview, Belleair, Fla.

Some of these hotels had remarkable features and amenities for their time:

<u>The Tampa Bay Hotel</u>- with the success of Flagler's Ponce de Leon Hotel in St. Augustine, Plant decided that Tampa needed a spectacular new hotel. With the agreement of the town council for a new bridge across the Hillsborough River and for substantial real estate tax abatement, Plant chose New York City architect John A. Wood who also designed the Hillsborough County Courthouse, the Piney Woods Hotel, Oglethorpe Hotel, Mizzen Top Hotel and Grand Hotel. The cornerstone was laid on July 26, 1888 and the 511-room Tampa Bay Hotel opened on February 5, 1891 with a 70 square foot lobby and a 23-foot high rotunda supported by thirteen granite columns. Florida's first fully electrified hotel contained the following features:

1. Guest rooms: one bathroom for every three rooms (while Flagler's Ponce de Leon had shared bathrooms at the end of the hallways); carpets, soft beds, telephones, hot water heating, a fireplace and circular fifteen-inch diameter mirror set in the ceiling of each room with three bulbs set below to throw out light to all parts of the rooms. In addition, there were two electric lights placed in the side of the dressing table.
2. Sixteen suites: each with double parlors, three bedrooms, sliding doors, two bathrooms and private hallways.
3. Public facilities included a cafe, billiard room, telegraph office, barber shop, drug store, flower shop and special ladies area for shuffleboards, billiards and cafe facilities. Also available were needle and mineral water baths, massages and a physician. There were other small shops in an arcade area.

4. Recreation facilities included tennis and croquet courts, rickshaw rides, an 18-hole golf course, stables, hunting trips and excursions by electric launch on the Hillsborough River to observe alligators and mullet, and, after returning to the hotel, tea and crackers at 5:00 PM.

5. Evening meals served from 6:00 PM were formal with fancy dresses, jackets and ties. There was live music by the orchestra located on the second level of the large dining room. After dinner, the guests separated, men to the bar for stories, cigars and after-dinner liqueurs, women to the sitting room for cool drinks and conversation.

6. Another service provided by the hotel were fifteen dog kennels for the accommodation of pets carried along by hotel guests during their stay in Florida. The kennels were located in a half-acre park with shade trees and enclosed by a six foot fence. The hotel's brochure claimed that it had "the most complete dog accommodations of any hotel in existence."

In the 1896-97 season, Plant built a casino/auditorium: an 80 x 110 foot exhibition building with a clubhouse in the front and a combined auditorium and swimming pool in the rear. The eastern end of the clubhouse contained two bowling alleys and a shuffleboard court. When needed as an auditorium, the tiled pool could be covered with a wooden floor. When the hall, which seated 1,800 persons, was not used as a theater, the dressing rooms of the actors became changing rooms for the bathers. The hotel had great wide verandas, beautiful gardens, arches of electric light, oriental ceramics, beautiful statues and paintings, Turkish rugs, Chinese bronze vases. Mr. and Mrs. Plant took trips to Europe and the Far East to select and purchase articles to furnish the public rooms.

A Tampa Bay hotel postcard of 1924 described the beautiful grounds as follows:

> "A jewel so magnificent should have an appropriate setting and so it has, in a tropical garden of rare beauty of foliage and species. The acreage surrounding the hotel should match its noble proportions and so it permits of orange groves, alluring walks, and enticing drives through long lines of palmetto and under live oaks trailing their gray banners of Spanish moss."

Alongside a small stream were planted many tropical plants and fruits including roses, pansies, bamboos, oleander, papayas, mangos and pineapples. Since occasional cold weather could damage tropical plants, a glassed-in conservatory was built to grow plants and flowers for guest rooms, public areas and dining room tables. After a trip to the Bahamas, head gardener Auton Fiche returned with a boat load of tropical plants. An 1892 catalogue of fruits, flowers and plants growing on hotel grounds listed twenty two kinds of palm trees, three varieties of bananas, twelve varieties of orchids and various citrus trees including orange, lime, lemon, grapefruit, mandarin and tangerine.

Even today, you can see why the Tampa Bay Hotel was the jewel of Plant's Florida Gulf Coast Hotels. Much of the original building is used by the University of Tampa and houses the Henry B. Plant Museum. When it opened on January 31, 1891, the journalist Henry G. Parker in the *Boston Saturday Evening Gazette* wrote,

> "The new Tampa Bay Hotel: It was reserved for the sagacious and enterprising railroad and steamboat magnate, Mr. H.B. Plant, to reap the honor of

erecting in tropical Florida the most attractive, most original and most beautiful hotel in the South, if not in the whole country; and it is a hotel of which the whole world need to be advised. The entire estate, including land and building, cost two millions of dollars, and the furniture and fittings a half million more. Nothing offends the eye, the effect produced is one of astonishment and delight."

Despite all the hotel's features, it was never a commercial success in Plant's time. He ignored the financial reports, subsidized the operations and claimed that the hotel was worthwhile if only to enjoy its great German pipe organ.

The Henry B. Plant Museum in the Tampa Bay Hotel (established in 1933) recalls the hotel's gilded age, when formal dress for dinner was standard and rickshaws carried guests through the hotel's exotic gardens. The Spanish-American War Room tells the story the hotel played in the 1898 conflict between the United States and Spanish-held Cuba. Because Tampa was the city nearest to Cuba with both rail and port facilities, it was chosen as the point of embarkation for the war. The hotel was designated a National Historic Landmark in 1977.

The Belleview Biltmore Hotel- Four years after opening the Tampa Bay Hotel, Henry Plant decided to expand his hotel holdings and acquired 700 acres at Clearwater Harbor. Plant commissioned architects Michael J. Miller and Francis J. Kennard of Tampa to design and build a luxury winter resort hotel on the Gulf of Mexico. From 1894 to 1910, Miller and Kennard had one of the most productive architectural offices in Tampa. They are credited with the design of several of the finest of the area's early buildings. Francis J. Kennard as born in London in 1865 and was educated there. He emigrated from England to Orlando, Florida in 1886 where he practiced architecture until 1894 when he went to Tampa. On January 15, 1897, the Belleview Hotel at Bellaire, Florida opened with 145 rooms, Georgia pine construction, swiss-style design, golf course and race track. The Belleview became a retreat for the wealthy whose private railroad cars were often parked at the railroad siding built to the south of the hotel.

The Belleview, named the "White Queen of the Gulf", was four and a half stories high and was the largest wood-frame building in Florida. In 1920, the Hotel was purchased from the Plant Investment company by John McEntee Bowman, owner of the Biltmore chain of hotels. For the next 87 years, the hotel was known as the Belleview Biltmore Hotel. It was listed on the National Registry of Historic Places and was famous for its Victorian charm and southern hospitality.

Many famous dignitaries were guests at this hotel including presidents George H. W. Bush, Jimmy Carter and Gerald Ford, the former King of England, (the Duke of Windsor) the Vanderbilts, the Pew family of Sun Oil, the Studebakers, the DuPonts, Thomas Edison, Henry Ford and Lady Margaret Thatcher, baseball legends Babe Ruth, Joe DiMaggio, and entertainers Tony Bennett, Bob Dylan and Carol Channing. In 1985, a $10 million renovation of the resort took place in the guest rooms and in the construction of a luxurious spa.

The Mobil Travel Guide gave the Biltmore a four-star rating and the *World Tennis Magazine* gave it a five-star rating for tennis resorts. The Biltmore was one of the few hotels to have a waltz composed in its name, "The Belleview Waltz." The Belleview

Biltmore Golf Club offered a beautiful 18-hole course designed by world-famous Scottish-born architect, Donald Ross in 1925.

The Belleview Biltmore provided 243 guest rooms in an intimate setting. In its better days, guests could enjoy a variety of guestrooms starting with a quaint one bedroom suite, all the way up to the 3,400 square foot presidential suite. Nearby residents considered the Belleview Biltmore to be one of West Florida's most picturesque landmarks. Banquets, meeting rooms, conference services, gourmet dining, and weddings with special attention to unique service were offered at this exquisite hotel.

Despite its membership in the National Trust for Historic Preservation's Historic Hotels of America, the Belleview Biltmore Hotel was demolished in 2015 after a desperate unsuccessful five-year campaign by the "Save The Biltmore" preservationists.

The Seminole Hotel- Two years before the opening of Flagler's Ponce de Leon in St. Augustine, the Seminole Hotel, a magnificent resort facility opened in Winter Park, Florida. It featured its own horse-drawn streetcar line, steam heat, a bowling alley, a billiard room, elevators, fire alarms, fire escapes, and a yacht basin. In the winter of 1888, the guest list included Ulysses S. Grant, Grover Cleveland, George Pullman, Charles F. Crocker and George Westinghouse. In 1891, Plant bought the Seminole Hotel and had it painted "Plant yellow" with white trim. The Seminole contained 250 rooms with connecting doors so that they could be rented as suites. The hotel housed its staff in a separate dormitory building and operated its own steam laundry. Seminole guests enjoyed tennis, croquet, fishing, horse-back riding and sailing on Lake Osceola. According to hotel advertisements, parents were encouraged to leave their children under professional supervision while they traveled to Cuba on a Plant Line steamship. Three years after Plant's death in 1899, the Seminole burned down and was replaced in 1912 by a new Seminole Hotel which was ultimately demolished in 1970.

Many of the employees of the Seminole Hotel who lived in Winter Park year-round acquired other jobs through their connections at the hotel. The majority of the hotel's business came during the winter months, leaving most employees free to seek other jobs during the summer months. Through their association with affluent white hotel guests, some local African-Americans procured off-season jobs maintaining gardens and orange crops for the wealthy people who returned north for the summer, leaving their Florida properties in need of maintenance.

The Inn at Port Tampa- designed and built by architect W.T. Cotter on the new wharf some 2,000 feet from the shore. The first building opened in 1888 with twenty rooms and the second structure added another twenty rooms in 1890. The Inn contained one large dining room and a smaller dining room for nursemaids and children. The Inn offered electricity, running water, comfort, convenience and entertainment. In a front-page article on January 29, 1891, the *Tampa Journal* described the Inn at Port Tampa as "colonial" and declared that the inn resembled a "cozy home" more than a hotel. It featured a large veranda on the ground floor which allowed guests to fish from the porch or from the windows of their rooms. The Inn was located nine miles from the Tampa Bay Hotel and built on piles far out from the main shore.

The Hotel Kissimmee- was built in 1883 with 125 rooms and opened as the Tropical Hotel on Lake Tohopekaliga. Isaac Merritt Mabbette, part-owner and hotel manager and contractor George

Bass built the hotel which was jointly owned by the South Florida Railway. Kissimmee was known as "The Tropical City" and in the 1870s featured a "ride-up bar" where horseback riders could drink their whiskey while sitting in their saddles. An 1897 brochure boasted "The hotel is beautifully situated on the shore of Lake Tohopekaliga, one of the loveliest bodies of water in the state and is particularly attractive to those who enjoy fishing, hunting and outdoor sports. No finer fishing and hunting grounds to be found in the state. The Hotel Kissimmee is homelike and comfortable, and the cuisine is excellent." In the fall of 1897, J. Hamilton Gillespie designed a nine-hole golf course, and within the next few years golf tournaments were being held on the grounds. When Plant acquired the hotel, he added rooms and changed the name to the Hotel Kissimmee. It contained public rooms with open fireplaces, billiards, lawn tennis and boating. Good hunting included quail, duck, deer, wild turkey and bear. A fire destroyed the wood frame Hotel Kissimmee in 1906.

The Ocala House- was built in 1884 and acquired by Plant in 1895. It was three-stories high with 200 rooms and with its extensive gardens and grounds occupied a city block. The guestrooms had working fireplaces, electricity, call bells and over-door transoms. The Ocala House provided a house orchestra for guest dancing. Like many hotels which featured some hunting and fishing, the hotel provided kennels for hunting dogs. The Ocala House survived until the early 1970s when it was demolished.

The Hotel Punta Gorda- opened in 1887 and was acquired by Plant in 1894 when he bought the Florida Southern Railway. The hotel contained 150 guestrooms in a relatively plain three-story structure but did provide steam heat, open fireplaces, call bells and a telegraph office. It operated only during the winter and provided dock facilities on Charlotte Harbor for guests arriving by yacht. Some of these included Andrew Mellon, W. K. Vanderbilt and John Wanamaker. In 1925, the hotel was acquired by Barron Collier and renamed it the Charlotte Harbor Inn.

It was renovated and a swimming pool was built along with two clay tennis courts for the famous Bill Tilden. Martin Fleischman assumed the mortgage in 1956 and named it the Charlotte Harbor Spa. After various owners, the hotel burned to the ground on August 14, 1959.

The Fort Myers Hotel- was built in 1897 by Hugh O'Neill with Plant as a likely partner. O'Neill owned a famous New York City department store and used the architectural firm of Miller and Kennard, the same company that designed the Hotel Belleview for Plant. The Fort Myers Hotel had forty-five guestrooms with separate bathroom facilities for men and women. The guestrooms were furnished with rocking chairs and white enameled head-boards and dressers. The Hotel operated a clubhouse on the Caloosahatchee River which contained a bowling alley, a billiard room, a shooting gallery and storage rooms for fishing gear and hunting guns. In 1907, Tootie McGregor, widow of Standard Oil executive Ambrose M. McGregor, bought the hotel, added fifty rooms and changed the name to the Royal Palm Hotel. Subsequent owners renovated and added rooms until World War II when the hotel was used as housing for U.S. Army soldiers. Finally, in 1948, the Royal Palm was demolished.

Plant and Flagler were friends who visited with each other on numerous occasions. A former mayor of Miami, John Sewell described them as, "best friends". They published each other's railroad schedules and advertised each other's hotels in their advertising and printed promotions. An apocryphal story illustrates their friendly rivalry. When the Tampa Bay Hotel opened in 1891, Plant invited Flagler to the opening events. When Flagler responded, "Where's Tampa?", Plant answered, "Follow the crowds". When Flagler built the Royal Poinciana in Palm Beach in 1894, Plant responded to the invitation, "Where's Palm Beach?" to which Flagler replied, "Follow the crowds." Most visitors to the Tampa Bay area eventually hear about nearby Plant City. This small city just east of Tampa styles itself as the "Winter Strawberry Capital," and backs up its claim with an annual strawberry festival. The city's name does not relate to agriculture, however, but to Henry B. Plant, the remarkable developer of Florida's Gulf Coast.

At the time of his death, Plant was a wealthy man and left a personal estate valued at between $40 and $70 million. The Tampa Bay Hotel never achieved the results that Plant hoped for. The City of Tampa acquired it from the Plant estate for only $125,000 in 1905. They lost money until it was leased to W.F. Adams who operated it successfully during the Florida real estate boom. At the start of the Depression, the City gave the hotel to the University of Tampa when it converted from a two-year community college to a four-year university. Some time later, the Henry Bradley Plant museum was created featuring a few of the old hotel rooms and many of the original Plant treasures. Plant's railway properties became part of the Atlantic Coast Line (now CSX) and most of the steamship properties went to the Peninsula & Occidental Steamship Company. The Southern Express Company became the Railway Express Co., now defunct, None of the eight Plant hotels are in existence except for the Tampa Bay Hotel which has been home to the Henry B. Plant Museum and the University of Tampa since 1933.

Plant's son Morton Freeman Plant (1852-1918), was the vice president of the Plant Investment Company from 1884 to 1902. He was part-owner of the Philadelphia baseball team in the National League and sole owner of the New London Club in the Eastern League. Morton Plant was a philanthropist who made gifts to hospitals and a one million dollar unrestricted gift to the Connecticut College for Women. His former 1905 mansion at 653 Fifth Avenue in New York is now the home of Cartier. It was designed by architect Robert W. Gibson. By 1916, Plant decided to move uptown because the area was becoming too commercial. Cartier acquired the mansion from Plant in 1917 in exchange for $100 in cash and a Cartier double-stranded necklace of 128 flawless matched natural pearls valued at $1 million (equivalent to $18.7 million in 2017).

As Christopher Gray of *The New York Times* wrote in 2001:

> "It's possible to walk by the Cartier Mansion, on the corner of 52nd Street and Fifth Avenue in New York City, without much of an idea of what it represents. A lot of people undoubtedly do. It's an impressive building – six stories of marble and granite, completed in 1905, in the neo-Renaissance style. The mansion sits in the shadow of a high-rise skyscraper – Olympic Towers – and, in addition to having been the New York home of Cartier since 1917, it's also one of the last remnants of a long-gone world that exists now only in fragments, along a stretch of Fifth Avenue that used to be home to some of America's wealthiest and most powerful families."

Henry Plant was a wily and resourceful individual. Though Connecticut-born, he became so prominent in the Southern business world (where he had his first major success in the freight transportation business) that he was appointed during the Civil War by the Confederacy to an important government position, collecting tariffs. In 1863, Plant managed to persuade Jefferson Davis (under the pretext of illness) to give him a safe passage document to Bermuda, and then, carrying a Confederate passport, made his way to France, where he talked the French into giving him a French passport describing him as a U.S. citizen living in Georgia – with which he re-entered the U.S. at the war's end. He then proceeded to amass a collection of fourteen railway companies (some of which he acquired during postwar foreclosure sales) and a correspondingly huge fortune.

By all accounts Henry Plant and his son Morton, who was born in 1852, were not close and when Henry died, he attempted to cut Morton out of most of his fortune by leaving the bulk of it to a grandson (this despite the fact that Morton was by then, and had been for some time, president of the railway company). However, Morton Plant and Henry's wife managed to successfully contest the will. Despite his father's doubts, Morton proved to be a good businessman. One of Morton's biggest pleasures was yachting and he was a member of several clubs, including the Larchmont Yacht Club, where he was a Commodore. He married for the first time in 1887, but his first wife Nellie died in 1913, at the age of 50. Only ten months later, the 61-year old Morton was married again – to the 31-year old Mae Caldwell Manwaring.

Mae, at the time she and Plant met, was married to Selden Manwaring, a hotel owner, and according to *Florida's Ghostly Legends and Haunted Folklore: The Gulf Coast and Pensacola,*

Morton Plant was so infatuated with Mae that he paid Selden Manwaring $8 million for an uncontested divorce. The society magazine *Collier's* observed: "Some little while ago, the country was agitated by a report that Morton F. Plant, a multimillionaire… was to marry the divorced wife of a restaurant manager. An interview was secured, and this statement given out by the great one: 'Yes, I am going to be married, and it's my own business.'"

Mae Caldwell Manwaring became Maisie Plant in 1914, and promptly moved into the premises at 653 Fifth Avenue. At the time, it was known simply as the Morton Plant House, and it was part of a cluster of mansions on that part of Fifth Avenue that been home to the Vanderbilts, the Astors, and others (in fact, the parcel of the land at 653 Fifth Avenue had been sold to Plant by William Vanderbilt; it had previously been the site of a Catholic charity hospital for orphans). The architect was Robert W. Gibson, whose other work included notable churches and cathedrals. He designed an opulent and decidedly unecclesiastic six-story home with an entrance on 52nd Street (the original address of the house was 2 East 52nd Street) framed by fluted columns and topped with an imposing triangular pediment. The building, then and now, radiates wealth and power, but it was also a monument to the exercise of wealth in pursuit of objects of connoisseurship.

Mrs. Plant came into her new life at a turning point in the history of Fifth Avenue, however. For many years, an ongoing battle had been waged for the character of Millionaire's Row on Fifth below 59th – on one side were the fabulously wealthy families (including the Vanderbilts) who'd built colossal homes there, and on the other side businesses and real estate developers who wanted the ideally-situated lots on which those homes sat. It was an inexorable and, as it turned out, inevitable change, but one that Morton Plant deeply detested, and he kept his mansion at least partly to thumb his nose at the commercial tradesman's storefronts.

The struggle was not one he was destined to win. The gradual shift in lower Fifth Avenue's identity had included the 1893 opening of the original Waldorf Hotel, on Fifth Avenue and 33rd Street and the Astoria Hotel in 1897 on 34th Street. By 1905, the St. Regis and Gotham Hotels were both up and running on 55th Street and Fifth Avenue.

In 1909, a French jeweler named Cartier came to town. Of Cartier's presence on Fifth Avenue, the *New York Times* would write in 2001, "As venerable as the jewelry company is, its arrival at the corner signified a bitter defeat for the mansion owners who first built up the section, some of whom were Cartier clients. When the building (the Plant home) went up in 1905 it seemed like a fortress against the advent of shops and stores, but instead it became an Alamo."

A major impetus for the establishment of a Cartier boutique in New York City was the presence of Cartier's arch-rival, the jeweler Dreicer, which is still located at 560 Fifth Avenue.

The Real Estate Record And Guide, July 17, 1917 wrote:

> "Mr. Plant was approached many times with offers to sell or lease his house, but would not consider any proposition until several months ago, when he decided that his stand against the trade was useless."

By 1917, life on Fifth Avenue and 52nd Street had long since become untenable for Plant. The ongoing encroachment of businesses, combined with the removal of virtually all the families to new addresses north of 59th Street, had left the Plants isolated both physically and socially. Plant had already begun work, the year before, on a new and even bigger residence, on 86th Street and Fifth Avenue.

The story goes that Mrs. Plant fell hard for a pearl necklace that had been exhibited by Cartier at its 712 Fifth Avenue address – this is the necklace that can be seen in Claudia Munro Kerr's interpretation of a portrait of Maisie, originally painted by the portraitist Alphonse Jungers (and which hangs in the Maisie Plant Salon in the Cartier Mansion today), in which she is wearing the necklace. It's really two necklaces: a double strand of enormous, natural South Sea pearls; the smaller is a stand of 55 pearls and the larger, of 73. The two together were worth $1 million – in 1917 artificial pearls had not yet reached the market, and creating a graduated set of flawless, large pearls took a lot of time and a lot of money. Pierre and Louis Cartier had both the necessary time and a great deal of money, but assembling such a necklace was a rarity and a challenge even for them.

Mrs. Plant wanted the pearls, and Mr. Plant wanted out of the house on Fifth and 52nd, so a deal was struck. The *Real Estate Record And Guide* reported on the resulting transaction in its July 21, 1917 issue:

> "The Morton F. Plant dwelling at the southeast corner of Fifth avenue and 52nd street, has been sold to Louis J. Cartier, of Paris, and Pierre C. Cartier, of New York, jewelers, who several months ago leased the property for their business. Ownership was transferred last Saturday for $100 and other valuable considerations. The option to purchase

was given to the tenants in their lease, and they have availed themselves of this opportunity. The dwelling is being altered for trade purposes and will soon be ready for occupancy by the firm, which is now located in upper Fifth avenue; it is opposite to the Vanderbilt houses, and helps to serve as a barrier to the northward movement of trade on Fifth avenue. Mr. Plant was approached many times with offers to sell or lease his house, but would not consider any proposition until several months ago, when he decided that his stand against the trade was useless."

So, Mrs. Plant got her pearls, and Cartier got its mansion. In keeping with its agreement with Plant, the exterior of the building was not altered in any way. Amazingly enough, after Cartier's 1917 conversion, the interior went virtually untouched, with the exception of a major refurbishment in 2000-2001. The building has landmark status in New York City and still looks substantially as it did when Cartier acquired it. Plant, clearly, had been looking for an exit strategy from 653 Fifth Avenue for some time, but Cartier and Mrs. Plant made it easy for him – he got out of a house he no longer wanted or needed: the Plant mansion on 86th Street would be even more palatial. It was designed by architect Guy Lowell. Morton, however, didn't enjoy his new home for very long; on November 4, 1918, Morton Freeman Plant passed away – less than a year and a half after the mansion sale – leaving Maisie Plant single, and extremely rich.

Virtually all the great Gilded Age residences on Fifth Avenue have long since been demolished to make way for more lucrative buildings. The last one below 59th Street to fall was the Vanderbilt mansion that occupied the entire block between 51ˢᵗ and 52ⁿᵈ Street, which was demolished in 1945.

In its Christmas 1947 issue, *Life* magazine ran a full page photo of the ground floor salon that shows what might be the consulting offices of an especially profitable private Swiss bank, under the headline "The House Of Cartier: It Sells Expensive Jewelry With An Air Of Dignified Disinterest."

Mrs. Plant owned and periodically lived in the Morton Plant House on 86ᵗʰ Street, for the rest of her life. She would marry twice more, before passing away as Mrs. Mae Caldwell Manwaring Plant Hayward Rovensky, in July of 1957, at the age of 75. By then, she had become a relic of a kind of unhurried, old-school gentility from which the world was rapidly moving on. The news of her death, and the auction of her estate, was covered in *Time* magazine, in a story entitled "At The End Of An Avenue.":

> "This week her Manhattan house, the last of the fabulous Fifth Avenue mansions to be fully occupied, will go on the block. Just to tabulate her possessions, the Manhattan auction house, Parke-Bernet, has published a 313-page illustrated catalogue. Sale of the 1021 listed items will take two weeks, and is expected to bring over $1,000,000, not counting the 167 lots of jewelry. Among the jewels are two of the most famous Oriental pearl necklaces ever assembled, a strand of 55 and another of 73 matched and graduated pearls, which in 1916 Mrs. Rovensky (then Mrs. Plant) received from her multimillionaire husband. Morton Plant had taken

them as payment of $1,000,000 for their house at
52nd Street and Fifth Avenue."

The pearl strands would sell for only $181,000 – they had, in fact, fallen precipitously in value just a few years after Mrs. Plant was given them, thanks to Kokichi Mikimoto's introduction of cultured pearls in 1916, and their subsequent explosion in popularity. The house on East 86th Street was torn down in 1960, and replaced by an apartment building – 1050 Fifth Avenue, which has, in its large lobby, some marble columns and a marble fountain that are the only remains of the Plant mansion. You can't help but wonder what Morton Plant would have thought about the fact that the only reason 653 Fifth Avenue still stands, in its entirety, is thanks to the very commercial forces he fled uptown in order to avoid.

Carl Graham Fisher (1874-1939)

In 1915, a real-estate developer stood on the corner of Lincoln Road and Washington Avenue watched the jungle of mangrove trees being chopped down and said, "Gentlemen, Lincoln Road will become one of the most beautiful shopping areas in the world."

That developer was Carl Graham Fisher, and the legacy of his accomplishments lives on to this very day, as indicated by the following list of developments and projects that he envisioned and then created.

- The Lincoln and Dixie highways. Fisher raised private funds for these two road projects, which were forerunners of the U.S. Interstate Highway System.
- The Indianapolis Speedway was built by Fisher, and the Indianapolis 500 is regarded by many as the world's premier automobile-racing event.
- Miami Beach.
- Fisher Island.
- Montauk, Long Island.

Carl Fisher was one of America's large-scale developers who envisioned entire new cities springing out of the ground. Born into poverty January 12, 1874, in Greensburg, Indiana, Fisher left school at the age of twelve to help support his family. Carl's failures in school were probably the result of his severe astigmatism. Early poverty and the limited technology of the time prevented his eye condition from being diagnosed and corrected until he was thirty-one years of age. However, his poor vision did not hamper his well-coordinated physical activities, such as running backwards. He often challenged and beat his friends who ran forward. A gifted athlete, Carl excelled at ice skating, swimming, diving, roller skating and bicycle riding. He set out into the world determined to make a mark for himself taking as his heroes Lincoln and Napoleon. The Civil War had ended only twenty years earlier with President Abraham Lincoln as a national martyr and former Indiana resident. From his earliest years Fisher was blessed with an uncanny ability for sales and promotion.

Competitive bicycling was all the rage at the turn of the century. Endurance races captured the imagination of the public, and were promoted by the fledging bike industry. Fisher joined one of the best-known bike clubs in the midwest, the Zig-Zag Cycling Club and made a name for himself on the racing circuit. Realizing the money to be made in selling bikes, rather than riding bikes, he opened his first bike shop in partnership with his brother when he was only seventeen years old. He advertised the business by creating a traveling race team led by a fellow speed demon named Barney Oldfied. Carl and Barney became lifelong friends. Carl persuaded Arthur Newby to build a new racetrack for bicycles and the six-day bicycle race tour. Carl realized that if he could get a major bicycle manufacturer to back him, he could increase his income by selling new bicycles. He visited George C. Erland in Columbus, Ohio who was one of Americas four leading bicycle makers. Erland was so impressed that he sent a whole carload of new Erland bicycles to display in Carl's new showroom. At nineteen years of age, Carl owned the finest bicycle shop in all of

Indiana. He embarked on a series of sensational promotions of the bicycles he wanted to sell:

- he rode a bicycle on a tightrope stretched between the roofs of two tall buildings on Washington Street
- he and his brothers built the biggest bicycle in the world and rode the twenty-foot high cycle through the Indianapolis streets
- that winter, Carl mounted a racing cutter built of steel tubing on runners in the Fisher shop and drove the streamlined snow vehicle along Capitol Avenue. No other sleigh could attain the speed of his lightweight cutter

Everything Carl did made news and kept his name on the front pages. Within a few years, Fisher had done well enough to transform his bicycle shop into an automobile dealership, the first of its kind in Indianapolis. There he created a multi-brand dealership where he displayed and sold Stoddard-Daytons, Packards, Stutz racers as well as REO trucks. In short time, the Fisher garage became one of the leading auto dealerships in the country. Carl's success was the result of an endless series of extraordinary promotions and hard work. Eighteen-hour days were the rule with Carl who had to be busy doing something all the time, according to Gar Wood, the inventor and acclaimed automobile racer. Fisher became a regular racer on the track with his powerful Mohawk automobile on which he sat unstrapped and bare to the wind. The car's engine was deafening, top-heavy and terrifying to behold. In 1904, *Horseless Age* named him among the best-known track racers. Fisher won races throughout the Midwest which led to an investment that brought his first fortune.

In 1904, Percy Avery walked into Fisher's dealership with a patent for a promising French device which consisted of a compressed gas cylinder filled with acetylene gas which was then used for lighthouses and buoys. It gave off an intense light far superior to anything in the car market. Among the many challenges to early motoring was the poor quality of auto headlights that relied on kerosene or candles. The real problem was that acetylene gas was extremely flammable and caused so many fires that no auto manufacturer would use it.

Fisher was a risk taker, however, and he put up the money to begin manufacturing this new, compressed-gas automobile headlight. The 1904 Packard was the first car to feature the new headlamps. Despite the light's popularity, a significant manufacturing problem existed, which was that the product's unstable chemicals frequently caused serious fires. When the Omaha factory exploded, for instance, a wire was sent reading, simply, "Omaha left at 4:30." Eventually the chemical tanks were made safer when they were lined with asbestos. With that change, Fisher's profits from the company soared. By 1913, the use of Prest-O-Lite headlights were nationwide, and caught the attention of the Union Carbide Company. Nine years after Fisher started the company, a deal was struck and Prest-O-Lite was sold for $9 million; Fisher's share was $6 million. With that bankroll in hand, the 43-year old Fisher began to look for even bigger, and more exciting projects on which to lavish his considerable skills and his newly-acquired fortune.

Next, he pursued his dream of building a major American automobile racetrack. On a 1905 trip overseas to compete in France's James Gordon Bennett Cup Races, Fisher was stunned by the European cars superiority over the U.S. models, noting that they could "go uphill faster than the American cars can come down." Fisher wrote to Ray C. Thompson, sports editor of the *Indianapolis News* in May 1937 that.... "we had two very fast cars, but there was no place in America to test them over a continuous drive of more than two miles, and in order to test them even the two miles in Toledo, we had to hire special guards to do the work at daylight; and even this testing was stopped because the cars made so much noise on the boulevard. So, we went to Europe with cars that were very fast but with no place to test them at high speed for a continuous run of 100 miles or so... As a result, the French beat the tar out of us; in fact, we didn't have either car finish, and I could see that it was a lack of being able to test the cars over a continuous speed run. I made up my mind then to build a speedway where cars could be run 1,000 miles in a test, if necessary."

When he returned to America, Fisher set out to convince auto manufacturers that a testing track was essential to improve American-made automobiles and that Indianapolis was the logical location for such a track. Incredibly, of the more than one hundred different cars manufactured in Indiana, only sixteen survived for fifteen years: American, Apperson, Auburn, Cole, Davis, Duesenberg, Elcar, Empire, Haynes, Lexington, Marmon, Maxwell, McFarlan, Studebaker, Stutz and Waverley Electric.

Fisher gained the support of Tom Taggert, three-time mayor of Indianapolis who proposed that the track be built at French Lick Springs, Indiana where he was building a new hotel and spa. Unfortunately, there was insufficient land available for the racetrack.

Finally, in 1909, on the old Pressley farm, five miles northwest of Indianapolis, Fisher and his partners, Arthur C. Newby of the National Motor Vehicle Company, Frank H. Wheeler of the Wheeler-Schebler Carburetor Company and Jim Allison invested $250,000 and built a two-and-a-half-mile oval track for automobile racing: the Indianapolis Speedway.

Cars, however, were not the first machines to race at the Speedway, which was originally paved with crushed stone. Instead, motorcycles tested the new track's fitness. The motorcyclists didn't know what to make of the facility when they came to Indianapolis in August 1909. The two-wheel daredevils were used to small board tracks, and seemed intimidated by the Indianapolis raceway's long straightaways and monstrous curves. On August 19, 1909, a week after the motorcyclists had tried their luck, the first automobile races were run at the Speedway. The results were immediately deadly; six people were killed, including three drivers. Fisher stopped the race after 235 miles of the scheduled 300 miles had been completed.

The crushed stone track proved unsuitable for racing, so Fisher returned to the drawing board. He convinced his associate, Arthur C. Newby, to pay for repaving the track with 3,200,000 ten-pound bricks and "The Brickyard" was born. The new surface stood up well during the 1910 racing season, and Fisher promised bigger things to come for the next year. On Memorial Day in 1911, the Speedway hosted the first in its long tradition of 500-mile races. Ray Harroun, driving an Indianapolis-made Marmon Wasp, won the race with an average speed of 74.59 miles per hour. Fisher had helped inaugurate an event that became known as "the greatest spectacle in racing," and he drove the first Indianapolis 500 pace car- a Stoddard Dayton.

Fisher next turned his restless energy to a problem that had plagued the automobile industry for years, namely, bad roads. Driving an automobile in those days was a real adventure as motorists not only had to deal with inadequate roads but also a lack of directional signs. Drake Hokanson, in his history of the Lincoln Highway, pointed out that the 180,000 registered motor vehicles in the United States in 1910 had only 2.5 million miles of road to drive on (with only 7 percent of those miles improved in any manner).

"The highways of America," Fisher wrote to his friend, author Elbert Hubbard, "are built chiefly of politics, whereas the proper material is crushed rock or concrete." Fisher met the road problem like he did any other problem: head on. At a September 1912 dinner party for automobile manufacturers at the Deutsches Haus in Indianapolis, Fisher unveiled his plan for a highway spanning the country from New York City to California, "A road across the United States! Let's build it before we're too old to enjoy it!", Fisher urged the auto executives. His idea was to build a coast-to-coast highway in time for the May 1915 Panama-Pacific International Exposition in San Francisco. Fisher estimated that a transcontinental highway would cost $10 million, and he sought pledges from the automobile executives present at the dinner. Just 30 minutes after his talk, Fisher received $300,000 from Frank A. Seiberling, of the Goodyear Company, who pledged the amount even without first checking with his board of directors.

A few months after the Indianapolis dinner, Fisher received a letter from Henry Joy, Packard Motor Company president, pledging $150,000 for the proposed roadway. Joy, a leading force behind getting the coast-to-coast highway built, suggested that the road be named for Abraham Lincoln. On July 1, 1913, the Lincoln

Highway Association was created with Joy as president and Fisher as vice president. The association's goal was to:

> ... procure the establishment of a continuous improved highway from the Atlantic to the Pacific, open to lawful traffic of all description without toll charges: such highway to be known in memory of Abraham Lincoln, as "The Lincoln Highway."

Fisher, as he had for his other ventures, employed a direct method for raising money. He wrote one Lincoln Highway Association official that it was easy to get contributions from people. "You should first give them a good dinner, then a good cussing, whenever you want money," Fisher explained. Although this technique worked with most people, it did not work with one of America's leading automobile manufacturers- Henry Ford. Despite requests from U.S. Senator Albert Beveridge, Thomas Edison, and Elbert Hubbard, all close Ford friends, and a personal appeal from Fisher, Ford refused to give any financial assistance to the Lincoln Highway. He declared it was the government's responsibility, not private citizens, to build better roads. The association announced the Lincoln Highway's intended route at the annual governors' conference in Colorado in late August 1913. The planned route ran for 3,389 miles, from Times Square in New York to Lincoln Park in San Francisco and passed through New Jersey, Pennsylvania, Ohio, Indiana, Illinois, Iowa, Nebraska, Wyoming, Utah, Nevada, and California. As work progressed on the first U.S. transcontinental highway, Fisher turned his sights elsewhere, especially to improving a jungle of swamps to be known as Miami Beach.

Although Fisher had big dreams for Miami Beach, his wife, Jane, was not impressed with the area on their first trip in 1912. Mosquitoes blackened the couple's clothing and Jane "refused to find any charm in this deserted strip of ugly land rimmed with a sandy beach." Carl, however, had a grander vision: "Look, honey," he told his wife, "I'm going to build a city here! A city like magic, like romantic places you read and dream about, but never see."

Florida, as Fisher envisioned the state, could be the perfect vacation spot for Northern-based automobile owners and their families who wished to escape harsh winter weather. To get vacationers to his resort, Fisher, the "father of the Lincoln Highway," had to use his promotional talents once again to nurture another highway's birth. On December 4, 1914, he wrote to Indiana Governor Samuel Ralston and suggested that the Dixie Highway from Indiana to Florida would "do more good for the South than if they should get ten cents for their cotton." The highway could also "mean hundreds of millions of dollars to Indiana in the next 25 years." Fisher offered his promotional skills on the road's behalf, leading 15 cars from Indianapolis to Miami on a Dixie Highway Pathfinding Tour. In September 1916, Fisher and Ralston attended a celebration in Martinsville that marked the opening of the roadway from Indianapolis to Miami.

Throughout Fisher's early years he showed a keen eye for identifying potentially valuable real estate. He also appreciated the importance of using quality materials and the best construction techniques, and so his showrooms, offices, plants and homes were showplaces. In 1913, he applied his appreciation for real estate and construction to a project that thrust him into the ranks of the country's leading real estate czars.

While vacationing in south Florida, Fisher couldn't help but notice the barrier island that paralleled the city of Miami. Miami Beach, as it was called, comprised 3,500 acres of dense mangrove swamps and beach. In 1912, Miami Beach was just a remote and inaccessible peninsula. Three different companies were selling land for homesites without much success. In northern Miami Beach, Quaker John Collins and his son-in-law Thomas Pancoast were trying to promote a hotel site: "Facing 600 feet along the Atlantic Ocean. Special inducements and liberal terms to parties who will erect the class of hotel desired." (Advertisement in the *Miami Metropolis*, March 21, 1914).

After Henry Flagler's Florida East Coast Railroad was extended through Miami to Key West, it is not surprising that the Collins and Pancoast families created the Miami Beach Improvement Company. John Collins realized that if Miami Beach was to become a popular vacation resort, access from the mainland by automobile was a necessity. After overcoming opposition by the Biscayne Navigation Company which provided ferry service across the bay, Collins finally received permission to build the bridge in May 1912. However, the actual building costs far exceeded estimates and the Collins family ran out of money less than a half mile short of Miami Beach: the longest wooden bridge in the world going nowhere. Collins' savior was Carl Fisher who had just sold Prest-O-Lite for $9 million. Fisher made a $50,000 loan to John Collins secured by title to 200 acres of land which became Fisher's first development on Miami Beach. Earlier, Fisher had purchased a lovely winter house on Miami's Brickell Avenue from Alonso Bliss who made his fortune manufacturing herbal medicines. The Collins bridge later became the Venetian Causeway.

In a relatively short time, Fisher single-handedly transformed Miami Beach into one of the most stylish resorts in the world. He cut down the mangroves and, to the astonishment of most observers, he dredged sand from Biscayne Bay to fill the swampland, and shipped in hundreds of tons of topsoil from the Everglades. He then built streets and sidewalks and laid out the city of Miami Beach with parks, golf courses, polo fields, lakes and canals. A "magic city" was created before the eyes of incredulous onlookers. Fisher also bought an additional 60 acres from the brothers J. N. and J. E. Lummus, who both headed local banks. While the Lummus brothers already carefully screened the purchasers of their land (lawbreakers were excluded, as well as African Americans), Fisher aimed to attract an even more-exclusive crowd. He wanted other newly-rich industrial magnates to vacation in Miami Beach. Several of them did, including Harvey Firestone and Alfred duPont. Working in Fisher's favor was the factor that new-money industrialists generally were shunned by Palm Beach's upper crust.

Carl Fisher built five hotels in Miami Beach— the Lincoln, King Cole, Nautilus, Flamingo and the Boulevard. He considered each visitor as his "paying guest" and would not have bell boys at the Lincoln, because he insisted that tipping embarrassed people. In the kitchen near the lounge stood an enormous refrigerator where meats and cold cuts were kept, so that when guest came in at night they could feel at home and "raid the icebox" free of charge. On each floor, a maid kept constant vigil on all guests' clothes. If a garment became wrinkled, it was pressed and returned without cost.

Fisher opened the spectacular 200-room Flamingo Hotel on the last day of 1920. He named the hotel after the flamboyant birds he saw on a visit to Andros Island in the Bahamas. The Flamingo

Hotel featured an 11-story tower with a jeweled glass dome. At night, multi-colored spotlights shone far out over the ocean, and were visible for seven miles. Fisher did not believe in locating hotels on the ocean side, and therefore, he built the Flamingo facing Biscayne Bay at Fifteenth Street on Miami Beach.

Fisher hired Charles S. Krom, a Colgate University graduate, as general manager of the Flamingo who remained in that position for twenty-eight years. Despite its success, Fisher wanted to sell the Flamingo. As he put it in a letter to a potential buyer, "Running hotels is not part of our business… We have a large amount of land to sell but we were forced to build the Flamingo." Fisher declared that with the successful tourism in Miami Beach, "we now need at least ten hotels with the capacity of the Flamingo." Fisher's overriding strategy for the development of Miami Beach was becoming clear: generate profits by enhancement of land values. The building of golf courses, swimming pools, polo fields and hotels added extraordinary value to the remainder of his real estate. Fisher's strategy to attract buyers of his unsold land was to announce that prices would increase of 10 percent every year. One of his real estate advertisement read: "If you wish to purchase property from us this season you may do so knowing the price will be advanced next year at least ten percent over the season. We try to give our customers an investment in a home site or business site that substantially and steadily grows in value." Nobody worked harder than Fisher to turn Miami Beach into a magical and profitable entertainment wonderland. In 1925, he sold $23 million worth of property. Fisher was at the apex of popularity and was often photographed with sports figures and movie stars. Since he was colorful and talkative, his interviews often made front-page news.

In the winter of 1921, President-elect Warren G. Harding visited Miami Beach and provided valuable publicity for all of South Florida. His landslide election helped to smooth the anxiety of the American people who has suffered through the horrendous loss of lives during World War I, the influenza pandemic of 1918-1919, President Woodrow Wilson's massive stroke, the Red Scare of 1919-1920 and the controversy over whether to join the League of Nations. Harding's platform of a return to "normalcy" and his good looks, charming personality and affable demeanor was a welcome relief for the American people.

Fisher made strenuous efforts to attract the new president's entourage to the Flamingo Hotel and finally succeeded when Harding and his wife Florence slept at a cottage on the Flamingo Hotel grounds. Harding played golf, posed with Carl's elephant Rosie, swam at the Roman Pools and spent two days sport fishing with Carl and friends. Harding even included a visit to the Cocolobo Club, Fisher's private fishing retreat, where he caught a sailfish. Before leaving, Harding praised Miami Beach in a public statement, "Because of the attractiveness of Miami Beach, I hope to come here again. This beach is wonderful. It is developing like magic." Fisher cold not have hoped for a better comment from the newly-elected President of the United States. Jane Fisher summarized her husband's coup: "Carl actually shanghaied the President right out from under the nose of the pip squeak Miami reception committee… The committee cooled their heels for an hour along the inland waterway waiting for President Harding to appear."

In 1923, Fisher built the Nautilus Hotel just west of the polo fields on the bay at a cost of $870,000 – considerably less than the Flamingo. As part of the development, Fisher dredged two islands from the bay, one for a pool and cabana area and the other for the radio station WIOD: Wonderful Isle of Dreams. Called Collins Island and Johns Island, they were connected by bridges to the Nautilus Hotel grounds. The hotel catered to wealthy guests with attractive guest rooms, beautiful furnishings and chandeliers, adjoining polo fields, stables and a gourmet dining room. For unique publicity possibilities, Carl Fisher used Rosie the elephant to carry building materials during construction, and later for appearances with children at Miami golf courses. During World War II, the Nautilus became a military hospital and then was converted into the original Mt. Sinai Hospital until it was demolished in the 1960s.

Fisher built two smaller hotels on Miami Beach: the Lincoln Apartments and Hotel and the King Cole Hotel. His last Miami Beach hotel was the Boulevard, his least expensive hotel, catering to a more middle class clientele and charging rates only 50% as much as his other hotels. Its cafeteria-style restaurant served plain American home cooking. The hotel was designed by architect William F. Brown in the Mediterranean Revival style. The Boulevard opened one month before the Great Hurricane of 1926.

Fisher showed extraordinary marketing intelligence in building hotels at least one block from the beaches. These locations greatly increased beachfront land values adjacent to his hotels.

As Polly Redford wrote in her book *"Billion-Dollar Sandbar"*:

> Carl's Miami Beach development was the first of its kind in Florida, the first to make something new, bright, expensive and fun out of what to most Americans had been nothing, a wilderness. Of all Florida resorts, Miami Beach was the best

publicized and most important, it best reflected the spirit of the decade that later became to be known as the Roaring Twenties… Carl and the Twenties were made for each other. Its interests- sports, cars, movies, radio, common stocks, speculation, real estate, Florida- were his too: its circus atmosphere- ballyhoo, publicity stunts, movie stars, flagpole sitters- suited him exactly."

At the end of 1921, Fisher posted a huge outdoor advertising sign at Fifth Avenue and 42nd Street in New York City which read "It's always June in Miami Beach." Fisher tried to get the other Miami hoteliers to join him and embark on a joint advertising campaign. Fisher wrote to his associate Thomas Pancoast, "I believe that this sign constantly standing out on rainy and stormy nights during the winter season would be of great value, as no doubt more people pass this corner than any other in the United States…. It would surely be a marvelous sign of great benefit to Miami and Miami Beach." But when the Miami Chamber of Commerce rejected the idea, Fisher proceeded to pay for the sign himself.

His other extravagant promotional efforts were mostly on target. The famous humorist Will Rogers wrote about Fisher's successful promotions, "Carl rowed the customers out into the ocean and let them pick out some nice smooth water where they would like to build and then he would replace the water with an island, and today the dredge is the national emblem of Florida." Rogers could always draw a laugh with his punch line about Fisher training mosquitoes not to bite customers until land sales were final.

By the late 1920s, many Miami Beach hotels and apartment building owners discriminated against Jews. Was Fisher anti-Semitic? Jane

Fisher rejected the idea stating that he once had been engaged to Emma Messing, a Jewish woman from Indianapolis. In addition, many of his good friends were Jews who were his customers, stayed in his hotels and enjoyed meals in his home. Other critics, however, said that Fisher believed that the "wrong kind" of Jew would be bad for business and therefore instructed his salesmen to refuse to sell to them or steer them to less desirable or remotely-located plots.

Segregation attitudes prevented African Americans from staying in Florida hotels and anti-semitism kept Jews out. Flamingo general manager Charles S. Krom wrote Fisher, "All convention people are naturally noisy.... I have never yet seen a convention that didn't have some Jews in the crowd and I don't believe a bunch of Realtors are going to be different from any other." Fisher agreed with this policy since his later hotels would not admit Jews, although he sometimes made exceptions for his wealthy Jewish associates. This "gentiles only" policy was common among Miami Beach hotels and apartment buildings through the 1950s.

Flamingo Hotel, Miami Beach, Florida   68

To provide guests with the fresh dairy products, Fisher brought 40 Guernsey cows from Wisconsin. Among its many features, the Flamingo had private docks, bath houses, and gondolas steered by Bahamians wearing brass earrings. There were also a men's club, broker's office, laundry, exclusive shops, and many other diversions. Fisher employed a number of gimmicks to attract attention, including importing a polo team from England, dressing young women in risqué bathing suits, and widely distributing publicity photographs taken at the hotel.

"The national press just ate that stuff up," says Howard Kleinberg, a columnist for the *Miami Herald*. "You couldn't pick up a paper in the United States without seeking a picture of either the elephant or some group of bathing beauties standing by the beach… Miami Beach all of a sudden became the place to go."

In 1923, Fisher expanded the Flamingo Hotel, adding sixty more rooms. At a cost of $870,000, the Nautilus, offered the ultimate for wealthy guests: posh rooms, and swimming pool with cabanas, beautiful stairways and chandeliers, a gourmet dining room, and, of course, the adjoining polo fields.

The increasing demand for rooms lengthened the tourist season and sparked a hotel building boom. The Lincoln Hotel opened on November 1 during the 1923-24 season, and the Wofford Hotel opened on December 6, 1923. Land sales and values escalated. In 1923, the Fisher-Collins interests sold a total of $6 million in real estate; in 1924, it was $8 million; and in 1925, sales almost tripled to $23 million.

By 1925, Miami Beach had 58 hotels with 4,500 available rooms. There were also new casinos and bathing pavilions, polo fields, golf courses, movie theaters, an elementary school, a high school, churches, and radio stations.

The dredges continued to pump sand, creating more land. Islands were created in the bay and sold to the wealthy. All of south Florida was booming. "Miami was transformed from a sleepy little town on the edge of Biscayne Bay into a Magic City of modest skyscrapers and legendary real estate profits" wrote Kenneth Ballinger in *Miami Millions*. Before long enough celebrities lived in Miami Beach to create a market for sightseeing buses. Guides used megaphones to identify the homes of the rich and famous. They could point out the estates of Harvey Firestone, Julius Fleischmann (Fleischmann's Yeast), Gar Wood, Albert Champion, Harry Stutz (Stutz Bearcat), Roy Chapin and C.F. Kettering (Delco). J.C. Penney owned a mansion on Belle Isle, and he brought classical pianist Arthur Rubinstein and violinist Paul Kochanski to entertain his guests there. The Fishers hosted Jascha Heifitz, Irving Berlin, Will Rogers, and George Ade.

Fisher himself was called the "Prest-O-Lite King," and he and his wife, Jane, were referred to as the "king and queen" of Miami Beach. "Nothing annoyed Carl more," wrote Jane. "He hated personal publicity. The only publicity he wanted was for the new city." On January 16, 1924, the *Miami Beach Register* noted that "Some day, if the migration of celebrities continues, it won't be necessary to publish *Who's Who in America*. The Miami Beach city directory will be all that's needed." The promotion of Fisher's tropical paradise sparked a Florida land boom. Six million people flocked into Florida in three years. By the end of 1925, Fisher was worth more than $50 million, but his personal life was in shambles. Devastated by the death of his only child in 1921, Fisher became a heavy drinker and womanizer.

By the mid-1920s, other developers began new projects. George Merrick and John McEntee Bowman were building in the Coral Gables community with the Miami Biltmore Hotel as its centerpiece. Further north, Addison Mizner designed and built the fabulous Boca Raton Resort and community. J. Perry Stoltz built the luxurious Fleetwood Hotel during the 1924-25 season and Newton Baker Taylor (N.B.T.) Roney, a New Jersey lawyer, built the largest hotel, the $2 million Roney Plaza on Miami Beach at 23rd Street. It was designed by architects Schultze & Weaver, who also were responsible for New York's Waldorf-Astoria and the Breakers in Palm Beach, Florida.

FISHER'S PLAN TO DEVELOP THE "MIAMI OF THE NORTH"

Always restless, with boundless energy, Fisher was no sooner established in Miami Beach than he started looking for his next great challenge. He found it at the eastern tip of Long Island's South Fork in Montauk, three times the size of Miami Beach and almost entirely undeveloped. It was 125 miles by highway from Manhattan. Fisher bought 10,000 acres in 1925, for the relatively modest sum of $2,500,000. He estimated it would take another $7,000,000 to develop it. "Miami in the Winter, Montauk in the Summer", was Fisher's slogan. He would provide the elite who had flocked to his Miami Beach, with a comparably exclusive summer resort just hours from the social centers of New York City and Newport, Rhode Island.

The original Montauk Point Lighthouse was authorized by the Second Congress under President George Washington in 1792. Construction began on June 7, 1796 and was completed on November 5, 1796. The lighthouse and adjacent Camp Hero were heavily fortified with huge guns during World War I and World War II. Those gun emplacements and concrete observation bunkers (which are also at nearby Shadmoor State Park and Camp Hero State Park) are still visible.

The Amistad, a Spanish ship taken over by slaves in 1839, was captured by the USS Washington near Montauk Point. The slaves were allowed to disembark briefly before being taken to New London, Connecticut for trial. The Amistad case was heard before the Supreme Court of the United States where John Quincy Adams successfully argued that the slaves had been kidnapped. Following the trial, the slaves were permitted to return to Africa. The case stirred widespread debate about the abolition of slavery.

Before Carl Fisher devised his Montauk development plan, Arthur W. Benson, the founder of Bensonhurst, Brooklyn, bought much of Montauk at auction in 1879 and relocated what was left of the Montaukett tribe from Indian Field to East Hampton. Benson planned to turn Montauk into a retreat for well-to-do sportsmen and formed the Montauk Association. The Association hired the famous landscape architect Frederick Law Olmstead to plan the development and had the well-known architectural firm of McKim, Mead & White design their summer cottages, some of which are still standing.

Carl Fisher had greater dreams than Arthur Benson to attract the globe-trotting set. Montauk would become a Sportsman's Paradise that was much in vogue with the very rich. As embraced by the gentry of the 1920s, a proper summer vacation consisted of vigorous outdoor activities centered around the main pursuits of yachting, fishing, golfing, hunting, shooting, tennis, polo and swimming. Naturally, it would be ideal if the prospective vacationers could pursue all those diverse activities in the exclusive company of their social and economic peers. In short, for Fisher's dream of a "Miami of the North" to succeed, he needed to construct a first-class destination that offered the litany of activities for the Astors, Vanderbilts and Goulds, as well as first-class hotel facilities. Diversity of activities in a socially homogeneous setting was Fisher's aspiration, and Montauk was designed to be that destination.

Montauk's 1932 promotional brochure emphasized the notion of social exclusivity: "Now Montauk Beach, through the vision and resources of a group of distinguished builders, is being transformed into America's finest out-of-door center, where the real aristocrats of modern America may find new health, new relaxation, new ways to play amid luxurious surroundings."

By the time Fisher arrived, Montauk was already well known among connoisseurs, as a first- class fishing and hunting retreat. Ever since the late 1800s, well-heeled hunters and anglers had gone "on Montauk" for extended expeditions. What they found was a beautiful, rustic outpost nearly untouched by the modern era. Teeming with geese, duck, turkey, fox, rabbit and deer, Montauk was a hunter's paradise. Inshore and offshore, no finer fishing could be found on the east coast. However, as a first-class resort – or a resort of any kind – it left nearly everything to be desired. Outside of a few private homes and a small inn that stood on the site of today's Montauk Manor, all that existed in the current downtown area was a hangar on the eastern shore of Fort Pond which housed a World War I observation balloon. On the shore on Fort Pond Bay, near the current railroad station, the village of Montauk crowded the water with fishing shacks, warehouses, commercial docks, and piers. In general, there was no electricity, no running water, no indoor plumbing, and little in the way of creature comforts anywhere in town.

Fisher was faced with the formidable task of transforming those 10,000 virgin acres into a world- class resort. Within weeks of his purchase, a crew of some 800 men were working around the clock, clearing roads, installing sewers, power lines and laying the infrastructure for a large scale, modern village.

Fisher ordered that an urban plaza be built with a seven-story building. He laid out all the roads in Montauk and built nearly all of them. He built glass-enclosed tennis courts near the railroad station (it is the Playhouse today), the palatial 200-room Montauk Manor, the Montauk Surf Club with its 300-yard-long wooden boardwalk, cabanas and Olympic-size pool. He even, in downtown Montauk, installed pink sidewalks some of which still remain.

Out of town, he built the Montauk Yacht Club. He created a racetrack (now Fairview Avenue) that winds its way around the Montauk Downs Golf Club (which he also built), and you can go on YouTube and you'll see one of the races held on that track. He built a polo field out toward the lighthouse and both the Catholic and Protestant churches on the roads he created in town. He built a group of stores east of the plaza that still stand, and Shepherd's Neck, a section of Montauk designed to look like a small English village (still there). He constructed about a dozen homes in the grand half-timber English style, and he brought in sheep to munch on the grass in the countryside. He also created a new railroad station for Montauk.

The Montauk Manor's guests could choose from a variety of daily activities. An oceanfront bathing pavilion, complete with outdoor pool and 1,600 feet of boardwalk along the beach, was constructed on the site of the current Surf Club. Eighteen quality holes of golf could be played at what is now Montauk Downs. Tennis players could choose from twelve outdoor clay courts near the Manor, or six indoor courts. For polo enthusiasts, playing fields complete with paddocks, stables, and herds of ponies were maintained at the nearby Deep Hollow Ranch. Equestrians could ride on established trails and the beach, and even run with the hounds in a traditional English-style fox hunt. Add to all that recreation the nearly unlimited fishing and hunting Montauk always provided, and it's easy to see how a visitor's day was filled. Established in his headquarters suite atop his new seven-story Montauk Improvement Building – at the time the tallest building on Long Island– Fisher watched his vision and plans become a reality.

Perhaps Fisher's most ambitious piece of engineering was the reconfiguration of present day Lake Montauk. It was, until 1927, a true lake – fresh water, land locked, and as such of no great use to Fisher. He needed a yacht club, with deep water berths capable of docking the grand vessels of the Astors, Vanderbilts, and Whitneys. Unfortunately, Montauk's only available anchorage, at Fort Pond Bay, was unsuitable- it was unprotected and subject to devastating ocean storms and high tides. Unperturbed, Fisher imagined the possibilities and came up with a grand solution: he blasted open a channel from Block Island Sound to connect Lake Montauk to the open sea. Once done, he dredged roughly half the lake to a depth of 12 feet and established the Montauk Lake Club on Star Island.

By the 1920s, Montauk was a cosmopolitan resort, a Monte Carlo on the Atlantic that attracted the world's elite. The 200-room Montauk Manor, designed by Schultze & Weaver, was the most luxurious hotel on Long Island, a favorite of the New York/

Newport crowds. Indeed, at the time, the Manor's popularity supported direct steamer service to Manhattan. Each night of the summer season, lines of fancy touring cars and limos would bring scores of wealthy visitors and high society who were bound for a champagne dinner and secret midnight rendezvous within the Manor's lavish guestrooms and suites. The Star Island Casino, next to the yacht club, was jumping every night, with fine food, excellent wine and the ever-present sound of money hitting the gaming tables. It was there that the then-mayor of New York City, Jimmy Walker, was nearly arrested during an infrequent raid by the local authorities. For the first few years, Fisher's dream city of Montauk was a genuine and profitable reality. Still standing in Montauk today are some 80 Tudor revival style buildings that Fisher built in the 1920s ranging from modest workers' cottages to grand hillside homes, a yacht club, inns, churches and schools.

Fisher had planned for everything, everything that is, except weather and the Great Depression. On September 17, 1927, a hurricane hit Miami Beach. Although the actual damage was not as severe as reported in media accounts, the news was sufficient to warn off travelers and the 1927/1928 tourist season was a bust. Then in 1929, the bottom fell out of the stock market and real estate values began a dizzying fall. Since much of Fisher's wealth was based on real estate, his fortune began to crumble. Within the year his empire had lost a third of its value, and the bankers who held his notes began to become nervous.

The Depression ended Fisher's elaborate plans for Montauk. Other developers planned various projects which might have succeeded had it not been for New York's autocratic highway and parks czar Robert Moses who later implemented the idea of encompassing the Montauk peninsula with parks: the 1,750 acres of woods, dunes and beach of Hither Hills to the west and the 724-acre Montauk State Park at Montauk Point to the east. There are trails through the tangles of bayberry, sumac, beach plum and shadbush, sandy and rocky beaches along the ocean and bay where migrating blocks of black ducks, Canada geese, old squaw and sheldrakes make their temporary homes. In addition, the 1797 Montauk Point Lighthouse continues to function above the ocean's rocks and waves. Power broker Robert Moses created one of the most beautiful iconic public works known as Jones Beach. Moses remembered Fisher fondly although he expressed relief that Fisher's 1920 plan to turn Montauk into the Miami Beach of the North had not been achieved.

As his credit began to thin, Fisher gradually sold his holdings – the Indianapolis Speedway, Miami Beach hotels, homes, yachts, land- that is, nearly everything that could be liquidated. Stretched beyond even his formidable means, his empire collapsed into bankruptcy in 1932. Three years later, Fisher declared personal bankruptcy. When he died in 1939, his personal estate amounted to just $52,198.

Although Montauk itself had a few good years in the 1930s and 40s, Fisher's dream of another Miami Beach was buried along with him. Without his considerable talent and salesmanship, Montauk was left with the imposing infrastructure of a grand resort, but with only a few of the details completed. Within years of its zenith, much of Fisher's Montauk fell into decay and partial abandonment. By the 1950s, his office building stood empty, the Montauk Manor was a brooding wreck, and his grand boulevards ran off to nowhere. Montauk's caretakers were left with no other choice but to fill in the gaps as best they could, the result being a somewhat uneven resort community.

Bird's-eye View of Montauk Manor and Tennis Court Building   Montauk, Long Island, N. Y.

Montauk today is an amalgam of Fisher's original vision of a getaway for the rich and the reality of an affordable vacation village. Admittedly, Montauk now has over 3,000 quality hotel rooms, some 50 restaurants, 1,000 deep-water boat slips, a world-class golf course, and some of the most beautiful ocean and bay beaches in the world. Even some of Fisher's original projects have been resurrected in the past few years. For example, the Montauk Manor and Fisher's seven-story headquarters building on the green are now deluxe condominiums. The yacht club is under new management, with restoration of its remaining Fisher sections in full swing. The golf course is better than ever, as is Montauk Downs. Many of the private homes Fisher built are still in use.

The Indianapolis attorney who often represented Carl Fisher, Walter Myers, remembered the last time he saw his former client. Visiting Miami Beach on business during the Great Depression, Myers spotted Fisher standing with one foot on a park bench. Myers walked up to Fisher, shook his hand, and asked him how he was doing. The answer Myers received from Fisher was not encouraging:

"I can tell you in a few words. The bottom dropped out of the sea. New York and Long Island took everything I had. I'm a beggar— dead broke, no family to fall back on. Yes, the bottom dropped out of the sea and I went with it.

You know, I promoted Miami Beach here. The grateful people got up a purse, $500 a month for me. That's what I live on. I used to make dreams come true. Can't do it anymore. I'm only a beggar now. The end can't be far away."

Fisher died from a gastric hemorrhage on July 15, 1939 in Miami Beach. Jane Fisher, who was divorced from Fisher in 1926 and thereafter remarried, never forgot her life with a man some Hoosiers had labeled "crazy." Living with her first husband, said Jane Fisher, was like "living in a circus: there was something going on—something exciting going on—every minute of the day. Sometimes it was very good; sometimes it was very bad. Still, it was living. It was excitement, aliveness, that I never found again."

Despite Fisher's extraordinary accomplishments, however, no beach, no highway, no hotel, and no race track is named for Carl Graham Fisher. Only Fisher Island bears his name. Fisher bought the island in 1919 from Dana A. Dorsey, a prominent black businessman in Miami who had given up on an effort to build a resort for blacks (who were barred from segregated Miami's beaches). The island itself was created in 1905 when the federal government sliced off the southern tip of Miami Beach to make a shipping channel from Miami to Atlantic Ocean. At that time it was an alligator-inhabited mangrove swamp. That lack of recognition would probably have been okay with Fisher since he always considered the project to be more important than his particular role in it. Dreaming, planning, working, and building were his most important values.

Although he had lost his fortune and later in life considered himself a failure, Fisher is widely regarded as a very successful man in the long view of his accomplishments. He was inducted into the Automotive Hall of Fame in 1971. In a 1998 study judged by a panel of 56 historians, writers, and others, Carl G. Fisher was named one of the 50 Most Influential People in the history of the State of Florida by *The Ledger* newspaper. PBS labeled him "Mr. Miami Beach."

Joe Copps, a long-time Fisher associate, said of him: "The reason Carl lost out was the way he did business. He wouldn't sell a lot until the project was completely developed. I believe Carl was the most honest man I ever met. He maintained that people shouldn't buy anything that they weren't completely sure of. He reserved the risks for himself."

Fisher's last years were spent at Miami Beach in near-poverty for him - $10,000 a year. People remember him as an amiable, informal old man who talked of great plans for the Florida Keys. He was a familiar character on the beach, dressed in Norfolk blazer and white flannel trousers. He was never without the floppy felt hat and perforated patent-leather pumps that had become Fisher trade-marks.

When he died in July, 1939, Miami Beach went into mourning, and the great of America came to pay last respects to the builder who had given so much to the projects he loved. Among the honorary pallbearers were Walter Chrysler, John Oliver La Gorce, Barney Oldfield, Charles F. Kettering, William K. Vanderbilt, James M. Cox, Frank Seiberling, Gar Wood and Bernard Gimbel.

Today, in a small park on the north end of Miami Beach, stands a bronze bust dedicated to Carl Fisher. It bears the simple legend:

"He carved a great city out of a jungle."

A Brief History of Florida's Other Hotel Pioneers

The end of the French and Indian Seven Years War resulted in the transfer of Florida from Spain to England. The colony was divided into East and West Florida. The British expanded Florida's agriculture especially cotton, rice and indigo. St. Augustine remained the capital of East Florida and Pensacola the capital of West Florida. By this time, native Americans from Georgia and Alabama were moved into Florida. They were called the Seminoles from the Spanish word cimarron meaning "outsiders" or "runaways".

During the American Revolution, Florida did not join the thirteen colonies but remained loyal to England. The Treaty of Paris of 1783 which ended the American Revolutionary War, allowed Spain to reoccupy Florida who forced the English settlers to relocate to the Bahamas or to England. In 1783, Spain reassumed control of Florida.

In 1816, General Andrew Jackson invaded Florida in pursuit of Seminole Indians and, in a brutal offensive, burned native villages, hanged two British subjects and captured St. Augustine and Pensacola. In 1819, Florida was transferred from Spain to the United States finalized by the Adams-Onis treaty. It settled a border dispute between the two countries and was considered a triumph of American diplomacy. Florida had become a burden to

Spain which could not afford to send settlers or garrisons. Madrid decided to cede the territory to the United States in exchange for settling the boundary dispute along the Sabine River in Spanish Texas.

Florida became a U.S. territory with Andrew Jackson as its first governor as reported by Florida's first American newspapers: *Florida Gazette* in St. Augustine and the *Floridian* in Pensacola. The Act establishing statehood for Florida and Iowa was approved on March 3, 1845 by the 28th Congress. The Florida plantation system with heavy dependence upon enslaved African Americans was continued. The Florida State Legislature created two colleges: the West Florida Seminary which later became Florida State University and the East Florida Seminary, later the University of Florida.

At the start of the Civil War, on January 10, 1861, the Florida Secession Convention voted 62-7 to adopt an Ordinance of Secession to withdraw from the United States, the third southern state to secede and to join the Confederate States of America.

The outbreak of the Civil War had a serious impact on South Florida with Union control of the Florida Coast for the entire war. At war's end in 1865, Florida was an amalgam of a mixed population of former soldiers both from the North and South, deserters from the Army and the Navy of both sides, a mixture of Spaniards and Cubans, recently-freed slaves, a variety of Indian tribes, so-called carpetbaggers and homesteaders, outlaws and renegades. Almost all of what would become Greater Miami was available to citizens or would-be citizens in 160 acre lots that the homesteader would live on and cultivate for five years which then could be purchased for $1.25 an acre.

South Florida's first real community of white settlers began in Coconut Grove when Charles and Isabella Peacock, settlers from England, opened a hotel in 1884. Coconut Grove attracted a wide variety of people: American industrialists, displaced Southerners, European nobility as well as Bahamian fishermen who called their settlement Kebo in Coconut Grove.

In 1891, a formidable Cleveland widow named Julia Tuttle, purchased 640 acres on the north bank of the Miami River and moved her family into the abandoned Fort Dallas buildings. Another visionary was John Collins, a New Jersey Quaker who began an agricultural venture on what would become Miami Beach. Collins started to build a causeway across Biscayne Bay to link the mainland to the beach which later became the MacArthur Causeway, a six-lane roadway that connects downtown Miami with South Beach.

About the same time, Geder Walker, an African American, built the Lyric Theater in the center of Colored Town on Northwest 2nd Avenue, Miami's "Little Broadway". By 1925, the area became known as Overtown with a thriving business district and several hotels including the Mary Elizabeth, the Calvert and Sir John Hotels.

DANA ALBERT DORSEY

The first black-owned hotel in Florida was the Dorsey Hotel in Overtown built by Dana Albert Dorsey. He was the son of former slaves whose formal education stopped at fourth grade at a school run by the Freedman's Bureau in Quitman, Georgia. After moving to Miami in 1891, Dorsey engaged in truck farming but soon began to invest in real estate. He purchased lots for $25 each in

Colored Town and constructed one rental house per parcel. He built many of the so-called shotgun houses and rented them out, but never sold any.

According to his daughter, Dana Dorsey Chapman, in a 1990 interview, her father's excellent penmanship was the product of his early formal education at the Freedmen's Bureau school during Reconstruction. Dorsey's business expanded as far north as Fort Lauderdale. He donated land to the Dade County Public Schools on which the Dorsey High School was built in 1936 in Liberty City. In 1970, its purpose was changed to meet the needs of the adults in the community by becoming the D.A. Dorsey Educational Center. In Overtown, the Dorsey Memorial Library which opened on August 13, 1941, was built on land he donated shortly before his death in 1940. Marvin Dunn in his well-researched book, *Black Miami in the Twentieth Century* reports that,

> "The Dorsey house was always filled with important dinner guests. Some of the white millionaires who visited were awed by Dorsey's accomplishments, achieved under difficult circumstances. Some even went to him for financial help. According to his daughter, during the Depression, Dorsey lent money to William M. Burdine to keep his store open. When Dorsey died in 1940, flags were lowered to half-staff all over Miami."

In 1918, Dorsey purchased a 216-acre island sliced from the tip of Miami in 1905 when the government dredged out a sea-lane from Biscayne Bay. His intention was to create a beach resort for African Americans because they were forbidden to use all other public beaches. After a few years when his efforts were rebuffed by the blatant anti-black racism of the time, he sold the island in 1919 to the Alton Beach Realty Company owned by Carl Graham Fisher who named it Fisher Island. It is now one of the wealthiest enclaves in South Florida.

DAVID LEVY YULEE

David Levy Yulee, born David Levy (1810-1886) was an American politician, railroad builder and attorney of Moroccan-Jewish origins. He served as Florida's territorial delegate to Congress and was the first Jewish person to serve as a United States senator. He founded the Florida Railroad Company and was known as the "Father of Florida's Railroads."

Levy added "Yulee", the name of one of his Moroccan ancestors, to his own name after his 1846 marriage to the daughter of ex-Governor Charles A. Wickliffe of Kentucky. He then became a Christian and raised his children as Christians but continued to be subjected to antisemitism.

Levy was born in Charlotte Amalie on St. Thomas. His father was Moses Elias Levy, a Moroccan Sephardic Jew who made his fortune in the lumber business. When his parents divorced in 1815, David came to Florida with his father and then enrolled at a boarding school in Norfolk, Virginia. He studied law in St. Augustine under the future Territorial Governor Robert Reid. David Levy was admitted to the Florida Bar in 1832 and began his political career as a delegate to Florida's state constitutional convention in 1838 and later became a clerk for the territorial legislature. In 1841, he was elected to the U.S. House of Representatives as a delegate from the Florida territory. When Florida became a state on March 3, 1845, Levy became one of its first new senators and the first

Jewish member of the U.S. Senate. He served as chairman of the Committee of Private Land Claims and the Committee of Naval Affairs. After failing to be reappointed, Yulee began to plan the construction of a cross-state Florida Railroad from Cedar Key on the west coast to Fernandina on the east coast which he described as "the Manhattan of the South" (complete with its own Central Park). Yulee was reappointed to the U.S. Senate in 1855 where his fierce views and heated speeches led to being called the "Florida Fire Eater".

Construction on the Florida Railroad started in 1855 with mostly slave labor struggling through swamps and dense forests. Despite near-bankruptcy in the Panic of 1857, the construction was completed in 1860. Soon thereafter shots were fired on Fort Sumter and the Civil War began. Yulee resigned from the U.S. Senate and returned to Florida to protect his railroad and supervise his plantations. He corresponded with Confederate officials including President Jefferson Davis and Secretary of War Judah P. Benjamin who was Yulee's second cousin.

The Florida Railroad was destroyed in the fighting and Union forces captured Fernandina on March 3, 1862. Yulee retreated to his plantation near Homosassa, Florida until it was captured by Federal troops in 1864 and then to his plantation near Archer, Florida. At the close of the war, Yulee was sent to Gainesville, Florida as part of a delegation to petition for readmission to the Union. He was arrested for treason against the United States and sent to Fort Pulaski. The charge of treason stemmed from a letter he had written before his official resignation from the U.S. Senate which urged Southern forces to occupy forts and seize munitions in Florida. His wife Nannie Wickliffe Yulee used her family's political connections to convince U.S. General Ulysses S. Grant to intervene on her husband's behalf. After being paroled in 1866, Yulee returned to Fernandina to rebuild the Florida Railroad. After he retired in 1881, Yulee relocated to Washington, D.C. where he died on October 10, 1866. In 2000, the state of Florida designated Yulee as a *Great Floridian* and the City of Yulee, and Levy County, Florida are named in his honor.

N.B.T. RONEY

The spectacular Roney Plaza Hotel opened in February, 1926. Built by Newton Baker Taylor Roney of Camden, N.J., the $2 million project was the first large luxury hotel on the ocean in Miami Beach. Carl Fisher's Flamingo Hotel was actually the first grand hotel in Miami Beach but it was located on the bayside.

N.B.T. Roney was a lawyer, real estate broker and builder from Camden, N.J. who was more interested in the hotel business than in law. He first visited Miami in 1909 on a trip from Cuba and returned in 1917 when he bought the Biscayne Hotel on Flagler and Washington Avenue. By 1919, he owned land all over the city and had bought out the J.E. Lummus land on South Beach. In 1920, he organized the Miami Beach Bank and Trust and two years later owned some two hundred shops on Collins Avenue between Third and Twenty Third Streets. In March 1925, he bought the unsold portions of Carl Fisher's Alton Beach oceanfront including his home, "The Shadows" for $2.5 million. Due to his quick deals and spectacular ventures, he became known as the "Man with the Golden Touch". Some critics called him "Newton Bath Tub" Roney or "No Back Talk" Roney or "Nothing But Trouble" Roney.

In 1924, Roney announced his plan for the Roney Plaza Hotel in Miami Beach on Collins Avenue between 23rd and 24th streets. He bought the site from T.J. Pancoast and John S. Collins in 1925. Roney hired the famous New York architectural firm Schultze & Weaver, later designers of the Waldorf-Astoria Hotel in New York, the Coral Gables Biltmore Hotel and Miami's Freedom Tower.

In 1926, newspaper advertisements announced the opening of the Roney Plaza Hotel with 15 acres of formal gardens, direct access to the beachfront, Olympic-sized swimming pool with high diving boards, oceanfront cabanas and gracious rooms. The Roney Plaza was a huge success drawing high society, Hollywood notables and European royalty. New Jersey Governor Morgan F. Larson, one of many politicians who stayed at the hotel, celebrated his three-week honeymoon during the 1920s. At the time it opened, the Roney Plaza was hailed as Florida's greatest hotel achievement.

Neither the 1926 hurricane nor the Depression prevented Roney from expanding and improving the Roney Plaza. In 1931, he added a pool with an adjacent cabana club. He sold the Roney Plaza in 1933 to Henry L. Doherty, a financier, oilman and utilities investor. Unfortunately, the life cycle of the Roney Plaza Hotel was short, only 42 years.

Over the subsequent years, with various owners, the Roney Plaza gradually deteriorated until it was demolished in 1968 and was replaced with Roney Apartments and Palace, a four-star beach resort and condominium apartment project designed by architect Morris Lapidus. E.J. Frankel, builder of the new hotel, created 1,162 apartments, described his prospective tenants as couples in their fifties and sixties with incomes of $25,000 a year or more who are new to Miami Beach and plan to retire here. He advertised that

> "for the price of a ninety-day vacation at the Doral or Eden Roc, they can have a year-round apartment, use it themselves whenever they want, and lend it to friends and relatives between times. For $700/month, they receive the same facilities and services set by big hotels. Morris Lapidus provides lush lobbies, lots of chandeliers, Olympic pools and patios, sun decks, shuffleboard courts, card rooms, game rooms, auditoriums and access to the beach."

Roney died in 1952. He left a rare map collection to the University of Miami in Coral Gables and a legacy as one of Miami Beach's most important developers.

ADDISON MIZNER

Addison Mizner was Florida's leading architect in the 1920s. He established his own Spanish and Mediterranean Revival style that became the architectural signature of Florida, and in so doing, created the ambience that transformed the landscape of South Florida.

A romantic and freewheeling man, Mizner was strongly influenced by the art of Spain and the Central Americas, where he spent much of his childhood. At the height of his career, Mizner designed more than 50 Palm Beach villas and Florida mansions for the nation's leading social families. He also designed the famous Everglades Club (1918) in Palm Beach, the Boca Raton Resort and Club

(1925) and the now-historic sites in Palm Beach: Via Mizner and Via Parigi.

A native of Benicia, California (near Oakland), Mizner grew up in a traveling family, thanks to his father who served as the U.S. envoy to Central America. The family eventually moved to Guatemala. In 1897, Mizner and Wilson, one of his four brothers, were lured to Alaska by the Klondike Gold Rush. Failing to strike it rich, the two brothers relocated to New York City, where Addison opened a shop on Fifth Avenue that dealt in colonial furniture and Guatemalan relics.

Although he had no formal university architectural training, Addison had studied design all his life. He took a job as an apprentice with a Manhattan architectural firm and served 10 years as a country house architect on Long Island. In 1907, he and a colleague designed a house in the Adirondacks that President Coolidge later used as his "summer White House." The 6'3", 280 lb. Mizner relocated to Palm Beach for his health in 1918.

The Everglades Club soon established his reputation as an innovative and exacting architect, and commissions for homes for some of the day's leading socialites soon began pouring in. Boca Raton soon saw the rise of Old Floresta, a subdivision that eventually featured 29 Mizner-designed, Spanish-style homes that still are well-preserved today.

In 1925, Addison was joined by his brother Wilson (who had established himself as a playwright, raconteur and entrepreneur) and the pair created the Mizner Development Corporation, with financial backing from such luminaries as Irving Berlin, W.K. Vanderbilt II, and T. Coleman DuPont.

In 1927, Mizner built a house for John R. Bradley called Casa Serena in Colorado Springs. Several of Mizner's friends got together in 1928 to publish a photo monograph of his work. It was entitled *Florida Architecture of Addison Mizner* and featured 185 photographs of homes. Paris Singer contributed an introduction and Ida M. Tarbell, the famous African American author, wrote the text.

But the brothers' timing could not have been worse because Florida's storied land boom of the 1920s was on the verge of a collapse. Before his company folded in 1927, Mizner designed the posh Ritz Carlton Cloisters Hotel Resort in Palm Beach, later called the Boca Raton Resort and Club.

Roney Plaza Hotel, as Viewed from Collins Park, Miami Beach, Florida

Mizner's map collection consists of twenty-eight pre- 20th century maps of the West Indies and Florida and includes works by famous cartographers such as Blaeu, Sanson, Popple and Homanno.

The Mizner name lives on. On the grounds of the Boca Raton Resort and Club is Mizner Lake Estates, a gated enclave of million dollar homes with 24-hour security. In Delray Beach, the Addison Reserve Country Club, a golf and tennis community, consists of 717 luxury single-family homes located on 653 acres. Also in Boca Raton is Mizner Park, an upscale lifestyle center with shops, rental apartments and offices. In March 2005, to commemorate his visionary contributions to the architecture of the city and state, an 11-foot-tall statue of Mizner by Colombian sculptor Christobal Gaviria was erected in Boca Raton at Mizner Boulevard and U.S.1. In addition, Addison Mizner Elementary School in Boca Raton was named for him in 1968. Addison and Wilson Mizner's series of scams and misadventures were sources for Stephen Sondheim's musical *Road Show* (2008). Previously, in 1952, Addison's friend, Irving Berlin, wrote a musical called *Palm Beach* which never got produced. In 1951, Theodore Pratt wrote '*The Big Bubble: A Novel of the Florida Boom*", which is a thinly disguised biography of Mizner. In 2014, Richard Rene Silvin wrote *Villa Mizner: The House That Changed Palm Beac*h about Mizner's own home on Worth Avenue and Via Mizner, Palm Beach.

Mizner, who also was an accomplished writer, published an autobiography covering his youth, and his days in Alaska and New York, *The Many Mizners*, in 1932, a year before his death in Palm Beach.

WALT DISNEY

Walt Disney's ties to Central Florida go back far before the debut of the Magic Kingdom forty years ago. His parents, Flora Call and Elias Disney, were married in Lake County in 1888 in the tiny Kismet church in the Paisley area of the county. The late *Orlando Sentinel* journalist. Ormund Powers wrote the following story in a 1998 column:

> "Walt Disney's maternal grandparents, Charles and Henrietta Call, lived in Huron County, Ohio, in the 1860s, and moved to Ellis, Kan., in 1879, but after several harsh winters, they moved in about 1884 to what's now Lake County and became Florida pioneers. The Calls' Kansas neighbors, Kepple Disney and his son Elias, also made the journey south and settled in the Paisley area. The Calls acquired 80 acres about a mile north of the Paisley settlement (then in Orange County). The Call children included a son, Charles Jr., and four daughters: Flora (Walt Disney's mother), Jessie, Grace Lila, and Julia.

> Kepple Disney returned to Kansas in 1887, but Elias stayed behind to wed Flora in a January 1888 ceremony in the little Kismet church. She was almost 20, Elias was almost 29. The couple soon moved to Daytona Beach, and their oldest son, Herbert, was born in Florida in December 1888. Later they moved to Chicago, where Elias worked as a carpenter. A second son, Raymond, was born there in 1890, followed by Roy in 1893 and

Walter Elias Disney in 1901. The boys' lone sister, Ruth, joined them in 1902. In 1906, the family moved to a 48-acre farm near Marceline, Mo., on the mainline of the Atchison, Topeka and Santa Fe Railroad, about 100 miles northeast of Kansas City. (Marceline is said to be the inspiration for the Main Street areas at the Disney parks.) In a few years, the family moved into Kansas City."

Back in Florida, Walt Disney's uncle Albert Perkins became the postmaster of Paisley in 1902 and served until 1935. (Perkins had married Aunt Jessie Call in 1887). Jessie Call Perkins taught in several Lake County schools and eventually served as principal of Eustis High School. When her husband died, she succeeded him as postmaster and served until 1946.

The story goes that the young Walt and Roy Disney visited Jessie and Albert in Florida during their summer vacations from school. If that's true, it must have been one of the bright lights for Walt in a boyhood shaped by hard work and harsh discipline. When Walt was 9, he got out of bed each day at 3:30 AM to help his father deliver newspapers in Kansas City, whatever the weather. Walt found enjoyment in drawing, even at an early age. One story has it that his first brushwork used tar, which was available on the family farm for patching roofs and fixing drains. The boy kept on drawing, encouraged by a gift of paper and pencils from an aunt and by a local doctor's kindness. Eventually, he enrolled in one of those correspondence-school cartooning courses- the kind you used to see advertised on matchbook covers- and when he was fourteen years old, he joined a Saturday morning class at the Kansas City Art Institute. That was 1915, and he was still just a boy. But in his drawings, Walt Disney had found a niche to fulfill his dreams.

Cora Wofford: At the turn of the twentieth century, she and her husband, Tatem came to Miami Beach to operate the Sea View Hotel. She leased the Breakers Hotel and sold some of her diamonds to renovate it. She then boosted the daily room rate to an unheard of $25 per day to attract the most affluent guests. It was so successful that she was able to build the Wofford Hotel adjacent to the Breakers over the next four years. The Wofford bridal suite was described as having "French windows looking out on the ocean and opening into a private Italian style balcony. The furniture is colonial ivory, and rose predominates in the artistic draperies and map shades." Unfortunately, Wofford's husband died in a hotel fire in 1927 while it was closed for the season. When Cora Wofford died in 1932, the hotel fell into disrepair and was frequented by organized crime figures.

Goodkowski Family: Built the Nemo Hotel in 1921 as the first kosher hotel in Miami Beach. The 100-room Spanish-style hotel was an example of a Miami Beach transformation from a decrepit $50 a week transient hotel in the 1980s to a popular South Beach restaurant by 2000.

P.J. Davis: Built the Marlborough Hotel in 1922 on Alton Road just north of Lincoln Road. After five years it was renamed the Mayflower Hotel by Peter Chamberlain who leased and managed it. Soon after opening, an advertisement appeared in the *Miami Herald* sponsored by development companies run by Carl Fisher, John S. Collins, Thomas Pancoast and James Snowden. Illustrated by sketches of the Marlborough and Flamingo Hotels, the ad reported the guests were sleeping on cots in the four large hotels in

Miami Beach, that the demand for hotel rooms proved that Miami Beach was a desirable vacation location and that ten additional large hotels were needed. Snowden, who built a prominent vacation mansion in 1917, leased it to Harvey Firestone. Later, the Firestone Estate became the site of the famous Fontainebleau Hotel, one of the most architecturally significant hotels in Miami Beach, Florida.

J. Arthur Pancoast: Grandson of John Collins, built the 122-room Pancoast Hotel to cater to a wealthy clientele. It was designed by architect Martin L. Hampton (1890-1950) who visited Spain in order to study Spanish-Moorish architecture styles. Hampton was well-known as a leading Florida architect. Among many other projects, Hampton designed the Hollywood Golf and Country Club, the Great Southern Hotel, the Variety Hotel, the Coral Gables Inn and Country Club, the Casa Loma Hotel, the original Coral Gables Biltmore Hotel and the Mirasol Hotel in Tampa.

Joseph Eisener: Carl Fisher's former land salesman built the Deauville Casino with dining rooms, entertainment, ballroom dancing, modern bathing facilities with lockers and rooms with private showers. Eisener sold the hotel to Lucy Cotton, a former Broadway showgirl who inherited $27 million when her wealthy husband was killed in an automobile accident. As Lucy Cotton Thomas Magraw Eristavi-Tscitcherine, she bought the hotel and named it the Beautiful Deauville. When she was accused of complicity with gamblers and gangsters, she leased it to health guru Bernarr MacFadden in 1933. He named it the McFadden Deauville, introduced health food and enjoyed modest success until the hotel was taken over by the U.S. Army during World War II. In 1944, Lucy sold the hotel for $750,000. McFadden meanwhile turned to politics and ran unsuccessful campaigns for the 1936 Republican presidential nomination, the 1940 Democratic nomination for U.S. senator from Florida and the 1948 Democratic nomination for governor of Florida. The McFadden Deauville was demolished in 1956 to allow construction of a new Deauville Hotel.

The *Miami Beach Register* in its January 16, 1924 issue wrote:

> "Anyone who is the least bit inclined to be a hero worshipper can have a wonderful time at Miami Beach, just watching the world linger here long enough to escape the cold of the north, to have a bit of paradise on this side. For in Miami Beach may be seen in the space of a season representatives of practically every nation, of practically everything worth while."

J. Perry Stoltz: A wealthy realtor who came to Miami Beach on his yacht in 1923, claimed in a 1924 newspaper interview, "Last year, I came down to Miami Beach only on condition that I forget business altogether and not buy a thing, real estate or otherwise. I succeeded fairly well, except when I went north in the spring, I found I was owner of 2,000 feet of bayfront…. between the Bay and Alton Road." Stoltz built the second major hotel on the bay and named it for his son, Fleetwood when it opened on January 15, 1925. It was 16 floors high with 350 rooms, a club room for yachtsmen and a roof garden for dinner and dancing. It was promoted as Florida's largest fireproof hotel. Like many early Miami Beach hotels, the Fleetwod had a short life, from 1925 to 1943 when it was demolished and replaced by an apartment complex.

<u>Samuel and Rose Jacobs</u>: Arrived in Miami Beach in 1924 where they operated a grocery store on Collins Avenue. Samuel took over the management of the Biscayne Collins Hotel and then constructed the Alamac Hotel in 1930. When it opened in January 1930, the *Miami Beach Sun* wrote about the Jacobs family:

"Walter, who managed the Alamac is the real 'minehost', Al does the buying for the hotel. Bob is a close second to Al. Miss Lucille is hostess at the Biscayne Collins Hotel. But its up to Pa and Ma that success is due."

When the Alamac was completed, it was referred to as being "in the quiet and secluded section of Collins Avenue at Thirteenth Street." All 65 rooms had baths and showers. The hotel restaurant featured Hungarian cuisine although the Jacobs family background was Yugoslavian. By 1938, the Jacobs had sold the Alamac and built another hotel with the same name across the street under the management of son Walter. The original Alamac became Ritter's Hotel owned by Rose Ritter and later was converted to the Revlin Hotel.

The Jacobs family operated the London Arms Hotel from 1932 to 1934 and built and operated the Tarleton Hotel as a kosher hotel until World War II brought U.S. Army Air Corps trainees to the hotel. After the war, it was sold and became the kosher Crown Hotel, then the Ramada Crown and now a luxury rental apartment building.

<u>William Whitman</u>: A successful Chicago printer during World War I, Whitman acquired Miami Beach oceanfront property and hired Chicago architect Roy France who designed the famous Art Deco Cadillac Hotel on South Beach in 1940. The building

was designed to look like a car, from its chrome center trim emblazoned with a glistening hood ornament, to the portico over the driveway, which resembled a car hood. As one of the tallest Art Deco buildings on the beach, the Cadillac Hotel was unique.

Whitman's son, Stanley, told how his father, met his 30-year younger wife on a Chicago street car and followed her to architect France's office where she worked. Leona Whitman, a Swedish immigrant, became one of the most important women in Miami Beach- financially as well as socially. When she died at age 97 in 1923, she owned more real estate in Miami Beach than anyone except Carl Fisher. Whitman was planning to create a Spanish village in 1922 in the heart of Miami Beach in a seven-block track. When Whitman lost interest in the development, N.B.T. Roney purchased the property from Whitman and created Espanola Way with houses, apartments and, as early as 1928, six hotels: the Espanola, the Village, the Guelda, the Ortega, the Segovia and the Mantanzas.

Pauline Lux: The daughter of a Pittsburgh glass blower, Polly had been a showgirl in the Earl Carroll and Ziegfield Follies and then the owner of a lingerie shop on New York's Broadway. In 1934, she relocated to Miami Beach with her mother and brother. In the next few years, she leased and refurbished the Trianon Apartments and the Luxton Hotel. In 1939, the *Miami Herald* claimed that she was the first woman to be licensed in Florida as a contractor. She built and renovated the Majestic, Imperial and Royal Hotels. Lux hired the famous architect Henry Hohauser to design a series of small hotels with retail shops at street level.

In 1951, Polly Lux married Miami Beach attorney and banker Baron deHirsch Meyer and became one of the most charitable people in the great Miami area benefitting hospitals, the Diabetes Research Institute and the University of Miami. She died in 1998 at 98 years of age.

Bernie Bercuson: Coming from Detroit and Windsor, Ontario in 1938, Bercuson learned the basics of the hotel business when he leased the Ocean Grande Hotel for the summer and was able to make a profit. When the United States entered World War II, Bercuson was hired by Ben Novack at the front office of the Monroe Towers until Bercuson was drafted into the Army in 1942. At war's end, Bercuson returned to work at the Atlantis, Ocean Grande and Sherry-Frontenac Hotels. Subsequently, he managed the Aztec and desert Inn in Sunny Isles, the Singapore in Bal Harbour, the Versaillas and Cadillac hotels in Miami Beach.

Harold A. Clark: Detroit and Miami Beach entrepreneur Clark built the Tower Apartment Hotel in 1935 for $1.2 million. With remarkable and unusual efficiency, it took only 60 days to complete the first four floors and begin accepting guests. A week later, the next three floors were completed and the final seven floors later in 1936. The fourteen floor structure opened as an apartment hotel then was sold and named the Mount Royal Manor Hotel. The 12/29/35 *Miami Herald* reported on the speed with which the building was constructed:

> "Ground was broken on October 15 and construction was started with skilled mechanics and laborers working 24 hours a day. Title to the property was obtained on November 13, but in the meantime, plans were whipped into shape and materials ordered. On November 28, a month prior to the opening of the hotel, the builders completed

pouring of the second floor slab, the first floor to be completed, and 12 days later the first floor slab was poured. During this period the steel for the upper floors was being erected and riveted and the building had been tiled in and all of the room partitions of the seven floors set in place.

Carpet laying in the first and second floor corridors and lobbies and the placing of furniture was started last Monday. At this time, the first, second, third and fourth floors are finished and part of the extensive landscaping completed. The fifth, sixth and seventh floors will be completed about January 10. The original schedule for the construction called for the partial completion of the building on January 18."

Henry Hohauser (1889-1963): Was born in New York City and educated at Pratt Institute in Brooklyn. He relocated to Miami in 1932 and practiced architecture in Miami Beach for more than 20 years becoming one of Florida's prolific architects. His firm designed more than 300 buildings in the Miami area and he is credited with being the originator of Art Deco architecture. Just a few of Hohauser's well-known buildings in South Beach are the Park Central Hotel, Colony Hotel, Edison Hotel and the Cardoza Hotel. His work in North Beach ranged from 1937 to 1954 and included streamlined curves, jutting towers, window eyebrows and neon decoration, signage and lighting. Many of his homes, apartment buildings, stores, restaurants, theaters and hotels are protected by the Miami Art Deco Preservation Society's efforts.

<u>Fred Humpage</u>: A longtime associate of Carl Fisher who became President of the Carl Fisher Corporation in 1939 wrote,

> "It is true, as you perhaps know, that there is a scarcity of ocean footage. Last year there were 47 new hotels built – most of them on the ocean front. This year there are 41 new hotels being built, and they also are built on the ocean front; but these hotels were not built by those who cater to the same class of clientele or guests as do the Pancoast, Whitman, Shoremeade, Braznell or the Carl G. Fisher Group of Hotels. The result is that the ocean front area has become very badly congested. Each one of these hotels that have been erected to occupy practically every inch of ground on which they are located. Such hotels as the Whitman, Shoremeade, and Pancoast are very much disturbed over the situation, as they will have next door neighbors, hotels which cater almost exclusively to Jewish clientele…"

Humpage went on to estimate that, as a result, property values would begin to decline. There's no evidence that they did. Instead, hotels continued to be built at a remarkable pace.

<u>Irving Cowan</u>: In early 1940, construction was started on the Shelborne Hotel which was designed by the architects Igor Polivetsky and Thomas Triplett Russell. Nine out of 13 rooms on a typical floor faced the ocean. In 1956, Irving Cowan lived with his new bride Marge in the penthouse of the Shelborne Hotel. Her father, Sam Friedland made his fortune with a chain of 450 Food Fair supermarkets. He developed the Diplomat as well as

the Shelborne Hotel. In 1958 Cowan said, "I've been in and out to owning the Shelborne two or three times. Prior to owning it now, when I looked at the property, the nostalgia got the better of me. But its turned out to be a good investment." Among the other owners of the Shelborne were the Galbut family of Miami Beach and Toronto investor Andrew Chung.

Morris Lapidus (1902-2001) was an architect, primarily known for his Neo-baroque "Miami Modern" hotels constructed in the 1950s and 60s, which have since come to define that era's resort-hotel style – synonymous with Miami and Miami Beach.

A Russian immigrant based in New York, Lapidus designed over 1,000 buildings during a career spanning more than 50 years, much of it spent as an outsider to the American architectural establishment.

Born in Odessa in the Russian Empire (now Ukraine), his Orthodox Jewish family fled Russian pogroms to New York when he was an infant. As a young man, Lapidus toyed with theatrical set design and studied architecture at Columbia University, graduating in 1927. Lapidus trained at the prominent Beaux Arts architectural firm of Warren and Wetmore. He then worked independently for 20 years as a retail architect with a specialty in store design before being approached to design vacation hotels on Miami Beach.

After his career in retail interior design, his first large commission was the Miami Beach Sans Souci Hotel (opened 1949, after 1996 called the RIU Florida Beach Hotel), followed closely by the Nautilus, the Di Lido, the Biltmore Terrace and the Algiers, all along Collins Avenue, and amounting to the single-handed redesign of an entire district. The hotels were an immediate popular success.

Then in 1952, Lapidus landed the job of designing the largest luxury hotel in Miami Beach, the Fontainebleau Hotel, which was a 1,200 room hotel built by Ben Novack on the former Firestone estate, and perhaps the most famous hotel in the world. It was followed the next year by the equally successful Eden Roc Hotel and the Americana Hotel (later the Sheraton Bal Harbour) in 1956 for the Tisch Brothers. The Sheraton was demolished by implosion shortly after dawn on Sunday, November 18, 2007.

The Lapidus style is idiosyncratic and immediately recognizable derived as it was from the attention-getting techniques of commercial store design: sweeping curves, theatrically backlit floating ceilings, 'beanpoles', and the ameboid shapes that he called 'woggles', 'cheeseholes', and painter's palette shapes. His many smaller projects give Miami Beach's Collins Avenue its style, anticipating post-modernism. Beyond visual style, there is some degree of functionalism at work. His curving walls caught the prevailing ocean breezes in the era before central air-conditioning, and the sequence of his interior spaces was the result of careful attention to user experience: Lapidus heard complaints of endless featureless hotel corridors and when possible would curve his hallways to avoid the effect.

The Fountainbleau was built on the site of the Harvey Firestone estate and defined the new Gold Coast of Miami Beach. The hotel provided locations for the 1960 Jerry Lewis film *The Bellboy*, a success for both Lewis and Lapidus, and the James Bond thriller *Goldfinger* (1964). Its most famous feature is the 'Staircase to Nowhere' (formally called the "floating staircase"), which merely led to a mezzanine-level coat check and ladies' powder-room, but offered the opportunity to make a glittering descent into the hotel lobby.

The Fountainbleau was once called, "the nation's grossest national product." The architecture critic of the *New York Times* Ada Louise Huxtable wrote in 1970 that a purple-and-gold Lapidus-designed bellhop uniform at the Americana Hotel in Miami Beach hit the eye "like an exploding gilded eggplant." When Lapidus designed the Summit Hotel in New York for Loews Hotels, critic Huxtable said that "it was too far from the beach."

Disclosure: I served as General Manager of the Summit Hotel from 1966 to 1970 and was impressed with its excellent design and layout as a mostly rooms-only 783-room hotel. Many of his innovations in lighting, fabrics and color have become staples of American design, in particular the design of hotels in modern-day Las Vegas.

Lapidus described his theory of design as follows:

> "I wanted people to feel something. If two people were walking by one of my buildings and one said to the other, 'Did you notice that building?' and the other said 'what building?' I've failed. But if he looks at it and says 'Oh my god' or 'that monstrosity,' I was glad. Because he noticed me."

Lapidus described his formula for success in the hotel business:

> "My whole success is I've always been designing for people, first because I wanted to sell them merchandise. Then when I got into hotels, I had to rethink, what am I selling now? You're selling a good time."

During the period before his death, Lapidus' style came back into focus. It began with his designing upbeat restaurants on Miami Beach and the Lincoln Road Mall. Lapidus was also honored by the Society of Architectural Historians at a convention held at the Eden Roc Hotel in 1998. In 2000, the Smithsonian's Cooper-Hewitt National Design Museum honored Lapidus as an American Original for his lifetime of work. Lapidus was quoted saying, "I never thought I would live to see the day when, suddenly, magazines are writing about me, newspapers are writing about me."

Ben Novack, Sr.: His dream of building the world's greatest hotel in Miami Beach, Florida began during World War II when the U.S. Army requisitioned more than 180 hotels and 100 apartment buildings in Miami Beach. As the owner of several hotels, Novack's contracts with the Army made him rich. In 1954, Novack built the Fontainebleau Hotel on an estate purchased from the heirs of the Firestone family for $16 million which made it one of the most expensive of its time.

Novack hired the Russian-born American architect Morris Lapidus at a bargain price to design the Fontainebleau. When it opened in 1954, critics lambasted the Lapidus designs, calling his architecture "pornography of architecture" and "boarding house baroque".

The Fontainebleau was the height of excess with woggles and cheese holes and a curved design which provides more guestrooms with an ocean view. Novack and Lapidus disagreed on many issues from the name to the design of the hotel. Despite the disagreements, the Fontainebleau Hotel opened on December 20, 1954 with pomp and ceremony and a $50-a-plate opening party for 1,600 guests. The hotel's La Ronde Room opened on Christmas Eve with Vaughn Monroe and his orchestra. In subsequent shows, the LaRonde hosted Frank Sinatra, Dean Martin and Jerry Lewis, Liberace, Elvis Presley and other famous entertainers. The James Bond movie *Goldfinger* used the hotel as its background. The Fontainebleau became and, to this day, remains Miami Beach's most famous hotel, so well recognized that until the 1970s there was no sign at the front of the hotel.

Morris Lapidus's relationship with Novack ended when he agreed to design the Eden Roc Hotel for Harry Mufson immediately north of the Fontainebleau. The Eden Roc was new and beautiful when it opened in 1955 and has remained one of the Miami Beach jewels.

Ben Novack, Sr. died at 78 years of age in 1985. He had operated the Fontainebleau Hotel for 24 years from the time it was built until it was sold in 1978. Ben's son, Ben Jr. and his mother 86 year-old Bernice were murdered in 2009. Ben Jr.'s wife Narcy and her brother were sentenced to life imprisonment for hiring hit men to kill Ben Jr. and Bernice.

ANTI-SEMITISM and ANTI-BLACK DISCRIMINATION

The 1940-41 Miami Beach Hotel and Apartment Book published by the Miami Beach Chamber of Commerce, contained 44 pages of hotel advertisements, many of which had such phrases as "Strictly Gentile Clientele" or "Restricted Clientele". The Pancoast Hotel advertisement stated, "Careful restriction of clientele assures congenial companionship."

Florida segregation laws against Jews and blacks as late as the Fifties covered many areas including schools, buses, public drinking fountains, trains, intermarriage, fornication with a white person, even that a black prisoner could not be chained to a white prisoner. Black entertainers starring at Miami Beach hotels and night clubs could not stay overnight at those hotels and had to find accommodations at Overtown hotels.

While Carl Fisher had wealthy friends who were Jewish and were permitted to stay at his hotels, other Jews were barred from his hotels such as the Flamingo Hotel.

A far-more publicized incident occurred in 1953 and unmasked the real reason blacks were not staying at Miami Beach hotels. It was intimidation. In May of that year, 164 black delegates to the Churches of God in Christ, Inc. were booked into the Betsy Ross

Hotel. The hotel's summer lessee, George Rone, chose to ignore the prejudice about blacks and deal, instead, with economics. He claimed that most of the convention business was going to seven unidentified major hotels. The others, including the Betsy Ross, he claimed were put in a situation where they needed another source of revenue and thus opted to house the black delegates. "There is nothing new in this situation," Rone told *The Miami Herald* in its May 3, 1953 edition. "Other hotels in Miami Beach have admitted Negroes attending conventions that were booked here by the city convention bureau."

Rone said "Delegates will not eat at the hotel, in fact, they will be here only for a little time each day," he said. "They will be gone from 10 o'clock in the morning until 10:30 at night. So actually, they will only sleep here."

Nevertheless, unidentified threats of violence caused the black pastors to cancel out of the Betsy Ross Hotel and move to Overtown. "It is one of the tenets of our church to avoid violence," host Reverend A.M. Cohen of Miami's Church of God in Christ commented. "Mr. Rone told us what happened, we decided against moving in." Rev. Edward R. Ullrich, president of the Greater Miami Council of Churches, called it "an unfortunate incident." He added: "delegates in any convention which is invited here should be treated with hospitality."

The following month, the National Education Association (NEA) was scheduled to convene in Miami Beach. As a result of the Betsy Ross incident, Tom F. Smith, Miami Beach's city convention and publicity director, was asked by the *Miami Daily News* if blacks would be accepted in Miami Beach hotels for that convention. The newspaper quoted Smith as saying the NEA had a firm policy of non-segregation written into its agreement to come to Miami Beach. "They (Negroes) will live in the same hotels as other members of their state delegations, but there will be probably only about 25 or so in a total of possibly 12,000 delegates. We have booked two Negroes into one hotel, four into another. They will eat in the hotels and will not use the beaches or any of the public facilities."

Two years later, in 1955, singer Harry Belafonte was the star of the opening night of the Eden Roc Hotel. Years later, he stated to TV interviewer Larry King that he was the first black entertainer to stay in a Miami Beach hotel. Whatever was the color line at Miami Beach hotels, it continued to crumble well before the Civil Rights Act of 1964. In 1961, former heavyweight boxing champion Floyd Patterson stayed and trained at the Deauville Hotel and in 1963, heavyweight champ Sonny Liston stayed at the Casablanca Hotel while training for a Miami Beach fight with Patterson that eventually was canceled.

Throughout Miami Beach history, there also continues the almost obsessive allegation that there once were signs at Miami Beach hotels displaying the particularly onerous language: "No Dogs, No Jews." While other restrictive language was common, there is no documentation that the specific "No Dogs, No Jews" sign ever appeared anywhere. Miami Beach activist Burnett Roth, an attorney and founder of the local chapter of the Anti-Defamation League, says no such sign appeared, and his experience with Miami Beach went back to the 1930s. In *Billion Dollar Sandbar*, author Polly Redford quoted Roth as recalling there was an apartment-hotel near Forty-third Street that had a sign that said: "Gentiles Only. No Dogs." Roth said he protested the juxtaposition of the verbiage to the city manager, who convinced the proprietor to change the sign. The words "No Dogs" were removed, "Gentiles Only" remained. Nevertheless, stories persist that the specific "No Dogs, No Jews" sign has appeared and that they have seen it, from the front desk of the Pancoast, to the Kenilworth (which had not yet been built when the sign ostensibly first appeared) to smaller hotels in South Beach.

Nevertheless, Fred Humpage's 1940 observation of the growing Jewish tourist population was not without foundation. In fact, it was most evident. The famous Grossinger name traveled from its Catskill Mountains resort in New York State to 1701 Collins Avenue when Jennie Grossinger built her Grossinger Beach Hotel there in 1940. It was designed by architect L. Murray Dixon (1901-1949), a native Floridian who worked in New York for Schultze & Weaver from 1923 to 1929. After he relocated to Florida, he struck out on his own and created Art Deco masterpieces such as the Grossinger Beach, Raleigh, Tides, Marlin, Tiffany and Victor Hotels. He was one of the first architects to build large-scale hotels with clean lines, sweeping curves, dazzling terrazzo floors, gleaming metal railings, shimmering etched glass panels, block and porthole windows. His designs personified the jazz age style of machine design, optimism and prosperity.

Ironically, the Grossingers later bought out the "carefully restricted" Pancoast and put the Grossinger name on it, selling its Seventeenth Street property which was renamed the Ritz Carlton and later, under legal duress, changed to the Ritz Plaza.

The Negro Motorist Green-Book

This series of AAA-like guides for black travelers was published by Victor H. Green from 1936 through 1966. It listed hotels, motels, service stations, boarding houses, restaurants, beauty and barber shops. Widely used when African American travelers faced a swamp of Jim Crow laws and racist attitudes which made travel difficult and sometimes dangerous.

The cover of the 1949 edition advised the black traveler, "Carry the *Green Book* with you. You may need it." And under that instruction was a quote from Mark Twain which is heartbreaking in this context: "Travel is fatal to prejudice." The *Green Book* became very popular with 15,000 copies sold per edition in its heyday. It was a necessary part of road trips for black families.

Although pervasive racial discrimination and poverty limited car ownership by most blacks, the emerging African American middle class bought automobiles as soon as they could. Still, they faced a variety of dangers and inconveniences along the road, from refusal of food and lodging to arbitrary arrest. Some gasoline stations would sell gas to black motorists but would not allow them to use the bathrooms.

In response, Victor H. Green created his guide for services and places relatively friendly to African Americans eventually expanding its coverage from the New York area to much of North America. Organized by states, each edition listed businesses that did not discriminate on the basis of race. In a 2010 interview with the *New York Times* Lonnie Bunch, director of the National Museum of African American History and Culture, described this feature of the *Green Book* as a tool that "allowed families to protect their children, to help them ward off those horrible points at which they might be thrown out or not be permitted to sit somewhere."

The inaugural edition of the guide in 1936 contained 16 pages and focused on tourist areas in and around New York City. By the U.S. entry in World War II, it had expanded to 48 pages and covered nearly every state in the Union including Florida. Two decades later, the guide had expanded to 100 pages and offered advice for black tourists visiting Canada, Mexico, Europe, Latin America, Africa and the Caribbean. The *Green Book* had distribution agreements with Standard Oil and Esso which sold two million copies by 1962. In addition, Green created a travel agency.

While the *Green Books* reflected the disturbing reality of American racial prejudice, they also enabled African Americans to travel with some degree of comfort and safety.

Victor H. Green, a Harlem-based U.S. postal worker published the first guide in 1936 with 14 pages of listings in the New York metropolitan area culled by a network of postal workers. By the 1960s, it had gown to nearly 100 pages, covering the 50 states. Over the years, they were used by black drivers who wanted to avoid the segregation of mass transit, job seekers relocating North during the Great Migration, newly-drafted soldiers heading

South to World War II army bases, traveling businessmen and vacationing families.

It is a reminder that highways were among the country's few unsegregated places and, as cars became more affordable in the 1920s, African Americans became more mobile than ever. In 1934, much roadside commerce was still off-limits to black travelers. Esso was the only chain of service stations that served black travelers. However, once the black motorist pulled off the interstate highway, the freedom of the open road proved illusory. Jim Crow still prohibited black travelers from pulling into most roadside motels and getting rooms for the night. Black families on vacation had to be ready for any circumstance should they be denied lodging or a meal in a restaurant or the use of a bathroom. They stuffed the trunk of their automobiles with food, blankets and pillows, even an old coffee can for those times when black motorists were denied the use of a bathroom.

The famous civil rights leader, Congressman John Lewis recalled how his family prepared for a trip in 1951:

> "There would be no restaurant for us to stop at until we were well out of the South, so we took our restaurant right in the car with us… Stopping for gas and to use the bathroom took careful planning. Uncle Otis had made this trip before, and he knew which places along the way offered "colored" bathrooms and which were better just to pass on by. Our map was marked and our route was planned that way, by the distances between service stations where it would be safe for us to stop."

Finding accommodation was one of the greatest challenges faced by black travelers. Not only did many hotels, motels, and boarding houses refuse to serve black customers, but thousands of towns across the United States declared themselves "sundown towns," which all non-whites had to leave by sunset. Huge numbers of towns across the country were effectively off-limits to African Americans. By the end of the 1960s, there were at least 10,000 sundown towns across the U.S. – including large suburbs such as Glendale, California (population 60,000 at the time); Levittown, New York (80,000); and Warren, Michigan (180,000). Over half the incorporated communities in Illinois were sundown towns. The unofficial slogan of Anna, Illinois, which had violently expelled its African-American population in 1909, was "Ain't No Niggers Allowed". Even in towns which did not exclude overnight stays by blacks, accommodations were often very limited. African Americans migrating to California to find work in the early 1940s often found themselves camping by the roadside overnight for lack of any hotel accommodation along the way. They were acutely aware of the discriminatory treatment that they received.

African-American travelers faced real physical risks because of the widely differing rules of segregation that existed from place to place, and the possibility of extrajudicial violence against them. Activities that were accepted in one place could provoke violence a few miles down the road. Transgressing formal or unwritten racial codes, even inadvertently, could put travelers in considerable danger. Even driving etiquette was affected by racism; in the Mississippi Delta region, local custom prohibited blacks from overtaking whites, to prevent their raising dust from the unpaved roads to cover white-owned cars. A pattern emerged of whites purposefully damaging black-owned cars to put their owners "in their place". Stopping anywhere that was not known to be safe, even to allow children in a car to relieve themselves, presented a risk; parents would urge their children to control their need to use a bathroom until they could find a safe place to stop, as "those backroads were simply too dangerous for parents to stop to let their little black children pee."

According to the civil rights leader Julian Bond, recalling his parents use of the *Green Book*, "It was a guidebook that told you not where the best places were to eat, but where there was any place to eat. You think about the things that most travelers take for granted, or most people today take for granted. If I go to New York City and want a hair cut, it's pretty easy for me to find a place where that can happen, but it wasn't easy then. White barbers would not cut black peoples' hair. White beauty parlors would not take black women as customers – hotels and so on, down the line. You needed the *Green Book* to tell you where you can go without having doors slammed in your face."

As Victor Green wrote in the 1949 edition, "there will be a day sometime in the near future when this guide will not have to be published. That is when we as a race will have equal opportunities and privileges in the United States. It will be a great day for us to suspend this publication for then we can go wherever we please, and without embarrassment…. That is when we as a race will have equal opportunities and privileges in the United States."

That day finally came when the Civil Rights Act of 1964 became the law of the land. The last Negro Motorist Green-Book was published in 1966. After fifty-one years, while Americas highway roadside services are more democratic than ever, there are still places where African Americans are not welcome.

BIBLIOGRAPHY

Abbott, Karl. *Open For The Season*. Garden City, N.Y.: Doubleday, 1950.

Amory, Cleveland. *The Last Resorts*. New York: Harper, 1952.

Armbruster, Ann. *The Life and Times of Miami Beach*. New York: Alfred A. Knopf, Inc., 1995.

Axelrod, Alan, ed. *The Colonial Revival in America*. New York: W. W. Norton, 1985.

Ballinger, Kenneth. *Miami Millions*. Miami, Florida: Franklin Press, 1936.

Barghini, Sandra. *Henry M. Flaglers Painting Collection*. Palm Beach: Henry Morrison Flagler Museum, 2002.

_____. *A Society of Painters: Flagler's St. Augustine Art Colony*. Palm Beach: Henry Morrison Flagler Museum, 1998.

Beebe, Lucius, *Mansions on Rails: The Folklore of the Private Railway Car*. Berkeley: Howell- North, 1959.

Berger, Molly. "A House Divided: The Culture of the American Luxury Hotel, 1825-1860." *In His and Hers: Gender, Consumption, and Technology*, edited by Roger Horowitz and Arwen Mohun. Charlottesville: University Press of Virginia, 1998.

Blake, Curtis Channing. *"The Architecture of Carrère and Hastings."* Ph.D. diss., Columbia University, 1976.

Boorstin, Daniel J. *The Americans. The Democratic Experience.* New York: Random House, 1973.

_____. *The Americans: The National Experience.* New York: Random House, 1965.

"The Breakers, Palm Beach." *Architectural Forum*, May 1927.

Brewer, Thomas B. *The Robber Barons: Saints or Sinners?* New York: Holt, Rinehart, and Winston, 1970.

Brooklyn Museum of Art. *The American Renaissance* 1876-1917. Brooklyn: Brooklyn Museum, Division of Publications and Marketing, 1979.

Bryant, Keith L. *History of the Atchison, Topeka, and Santa Fe Railway.* New York Macmillan, 1974.

Burt, Frank Allen. *The Story of Mount Washington.* Hanover, N.H.: Dartmouth Publications, 1960.

Bushnell, Amy. "The Noble and Loyal City, 1565-1668." In *The Oldest City: St. Augustine, Saga of Survival*, edited by Jean Parker Waterbury. St. Augustine: St. Augustine Historical Society, 1983.

Cable, Mary. *Top Drawer: American High Society from the Gilded Age to the Roaring Twenties.* New York: Atheneum, 1984.

Capitman, Barbara, *Deco Delights*. New York: E.P. Dutton, 1988.

Carley, Rachel. *The Visual Dictionary of American Domestic Architecture*. New York: Henry Holt, Roundtable Press, 1994.

"Casa Marina Inn, Key West Florida, Peter Gluck." *Architectural Record*, July 1980.

Cashman, Sean Dennis. *America in the Gilded Age: From the Death of Lincoln to the Rise of Theodore Roosevelt*. 2nd ed. New York: New York University Press, 1988.

Chandler, David Leon. *Henry Flagler*. New York: Macmillan, 1986.

Chernow, Ron. *Titan: The Life of John D. Rockefeller, Sr.* New York: Random House, 1998.

Colburn, David R., and Jane L. Landers. *The African-American Heritage of Florida*. Gainesville: University Press of Florida, 1995.

Commager, Henry Steele. *The American Mind*. New Haven: Yale University Press, 1950.

Covington, James W. "Alexander Browning and the Building of the Tampa Bay Hotel." *Tampa Bay History* 4 (Fall- Winter 1982).

_____. *Plant's Palace: Henry B. Plant and the Tampa Bay Hotel*. Louisville: Harmony House, 1990.

Curl, Donald W. *Palm Beach County: An Illustrated History*. Northridge, California: Windsor Publications, 1986.

Denby, Elaine. *Grand Hotels: Reality and Illusion*. London: Reaktion Books, 1998.

Donzel, Catherine, Alexis Gregory, and Marc Walter. *Grand American Hotels*. New York: Vendome Press, 1989.

Dorsey, Leslie, and Janice Devine. *Fare Thee Well*. New York: Crown, 1964.

Dunn, Hampton. *Yesterday's Clearwater*. Miami: E. A. Seemann Publishing, 1973.

Dunn, Marvin. *Black Miami in the Twentieth Century*. Gainesville: University Press of Florida, 1997.

Federal Writer's Project of the Works Progress Administration for the State of Florida. *The WPA Guide to Florida: The Federal Writers' Project Guide to 1930s Florida*. 1939. Reprint, with an introduction by John I. McCollum, New York: Pantheon Books, 1984.

Fisher, Jane. *Fabulous Hoosier*. New York: Robert M. McBride. 1947.

Fisher, Jerry M. *The Pacesetter: The Untold Story of Carl G. Fisher*: Lost Coast Press, Fort Bragg. CA. 1998.

Florida Association of the American Institute of Architects. *A Guide to Florida's Historic Architecture*. Gainesville: University of Florida Press, 1989.

Foster, Mark S. *Castles in the Sand: The Life and Times of Carl Graham Fisher*: Gainesville: University Press of Florida, 2000.

Frisbie, Louise K. *Florida's Fabled Inns*. Bartow, Florida: Imperial Publishing, 1980.

Galbraith, John Kenneth. *The Age of Uncertainty*. Boston: Houghton Mifflin, 1977.

Gannon, Michael, ed. *The New History of Florida*. Gainesville: University Press of Florida, 1996.

Gayle, Margot and Edmund V. Gillon Jr. *Cast-Iron Architecture in New York*. New York: Dover, 1974.

Gelernter, Mark. A *History of American Architecture: Buildings in Their Cultural and Technological Context*. Hanover, N.H.: University Press of New England, 1999.

George, Paul S. *A Guide to the History of Florida*. New York: Greenwood Press, 1989.

Graham, Thomas. *The Awakening of St. Augustine: The Anderson Family and the Oldest City, 1821-1924*. St. Augustine: St. Augustine Historical Society, 1978.

_____. *Flagler's Grand Hotel Alcazar*. St. Augustine: St. Augustine Historical Society, 1989.

_____. *Flagler's Magnificent Hotel Ponce de Leon*. St. Augustine: St. Augustine Historical Society, 1975.

Gregory, Alexis. *The Gilded Age: The Super-Rich of the Edwardian Era*. London Cassell, 1993.

Grismer, Karl. *The Story of Fort Myers*. St. Petersburg: St. Petersburg Printing Co., 1949.

_____. *Tampa*. St. Petersburg: St. Petersburg Printing Co., 1950.

Harner, Charles E. *Florida's Promoters: The Men Who Made It Big*. Tampa: Trend House, 1973.

Harvey, Karen. *America's First City: St. Augustine's Historic Neighborhoods*. Lake Buena Vista, Florida: Tailored Tours Publications, 1992.

Hatton, Hap. *Tropical Splendor: An Architectural History of Florida*. New York: Knopf, 1987.

Hayden, Dolores. *The Grand Domestic Revolution*. Cambridge: Massachusetts Institute of Technology, 1981.

Hepburn, Andrew. *Great Resorts of North America*. Garden City, N.Y.: Doubleday, 1965.

Jakle, John A., Keith A. Sculle, and Jefferson S. Rogers. *The Motel in America*. Baltimore: Johns Hopkins University Press, 1996.

Kalman, Harold D. *A History of Canadian Architecture*. Toronto: Oxford University Press, 1994.

Kearney, Bob, ed. *Mostly Sunny Days: A Miami Herald Salute to South Florida's Heritage*. Miami: *Miami Herald* Publishing Co., 1986.

Kleinberg, Howard, ed. Miami: *The Way We Were*. Miami: *Miami Daily News*, 1985.

_____. Woggles and Cheese Holes: *The History of Miami Beach Hotels*. The Greater Miami & The Beaches Hotel Association, 2005.

Koch, Robert. *Louis C. Tiffany: Rebel in Glass*. New York: Crown, 1964. 3rd ed., updated, 1982.

Kramer, J. J. *The Last of the Grand Hotels*. New York: Van Nostrand Reinhold, 1978.

Langley, Joan. *The Casa Marina: Marriott's Key West Resort and Addendum*. Key West, 1979.

Lapidus, Morris. *An Architecture of Joy*: E.A. Seamann Publishing, 1979.

_____: *Too Much is Never Enough*, New York: Rizzoli International Publications, 1996.

Lefevre, Edwin. "Flagler and Florida." *Everybody's Magazine*, February 1910.

Lenfestey, Hatty, ed. *Moments in Time: The Tampa Bay Hotel and Its History and Glory, 1891-1931, as Interpreted by the Henry B. Plant Museum*. Tampa: Henry B. Plant Museum.

Limerick, Jeffrey, Nancy Ferguson, and Richard Oliver. *America's Grand Resort Hotels*. New York: Pantheon, 1979.

Lockwood, Charles. *The Breakers: A Century of Grand Traditions*. Palm Beach: The Breakers Palm Beach, 1996.

Ludy, Robert. *Historic Hotels of the World*. Philadelphia: David McKay, 1927.

Lummus, J.N. *The Miracle of Miami Beach*, Florida: Miami Post Publishing Co. 1940.

Martin, Sidney Walter. *Florida's Flagler*. Athens: University of Georgia Press, 1949.

McGoun, William E. *Southeast Florida Pioneers: The Palm & Treasure Coasts*: Pineapple Press, Inc. Sarasota, Florida, 1998.

McLendon, James. *Pioneer in the Florida Keys*. Miami: E.A. Seemann, 1976.

Metropolitan Dade County Office of Community and Economic Development, Historic Preservation Division. *From Wilderness to Metropolis: The History and Architecture of Dade County, Florida*. Miami: Metropolitan Dade County. 1982.

Metzger, Betty, ed. *History of Kissimmee*. St. Petersburg: Byron Kennedy, c. 1981.

Miller, Floyd. *America's Extraordinary Hotelman Statler*. New York: Statler Foundation, 1968.

Moore, Charles. *The Life and Times of Charles Follen McKim*. 1929. Reprint, New York: DaCapo, 1970.

Mueller, Edward A. *Steamships of the Two Henrys: Being an Account of the Maritime Activities of Henry Morrison Flagler and Henry Bradley Plant*. Jacksonville, Florida: Edward A. Mueller, 1996.

Mullen, Harris. *A History of the Tampa Bay Hotel*. Tampa: University of Tampa Foundation, 1981.

Nevins, Allan. *John D. Rockefeller: The Heroic Age of American Enterprise.* New York: Scribner's, 1940.

Parks, Arva Moore. *Miami: The Magic City:* Miami, Florida: Centennial Press, 1991.

Parks, Pat. *The Railroad That Died at Sea.* Key West: Langley Press, 1968.

Patricios, Nicholas N. *Building Marvelous Miami.* Gainesville: University Press of Florida, 1994.

Pratt, Theodore. *The Flame Tree.* 1950; reprint, Florida Classics Library. Port Salerno, Florida, R. Bermis, 1994.

_____. "The Royal Poinciana, an Era's Grandest Lady." *Miami Herald Tropic.* October 29, 1967, 10-15.

_____. *That Was Palm Beach.* St. Petersburg: Great Outdoors, 1968.

Redford, Polly. *Million Dollar Sandbar:* New York: E.P. Dutton & Co. 1970.

Riis, Jacob. *How the Other Half Lives.* New York: Scribner's, 1903.

Rockefeller, John D. *Random Reminiscences of Men and Events.* Garden City, N.Y.: Doubleday Page and Co., 1916.

Roth, Leland M. *McKim, Mead, and White, Architects.* New York: Harper and Row, 1983.

Schwartz, Heather E. *Growth of Florida: Pioneers and Technological Advances:* Teacher Created Materials. Huntington Beach, Ca. 2017.

Shopsin, William C., and Mosette Glaser Broderick. *The Villard Houses.* New York: Viking, 1980.

Schlesinger, Arthur M. *The Rise of the City, 1878-1898.* New York: Macmillan, 1933.

Stern, Robert A.M., Thomas Mellins, and David Fishman, *New York 1880: Architecture and Urbanism in the Gilded Age.* New York: Monacelli Press, 1999.

Stilgoe, John R. *Metropolitan Corridor: Railroads and the American Scene.* New Haven: Yale University Press, 1983.

Strickland, Alice. *Ormond-on-the-Halifax: A Centennial History, 1880-1980.* Holly Hill, Florida: South East Printing and Publishing, 1980.

_____. *The Valiant Pioneers: A History of Ormond Beach, Volusia County, Florida,* Miami: Center Printing Co., 1963.

Tarbell, Ida. *The History of the Standard Oil Company.* 2 vols. New York: Macmillan, 1925.

Tebeau, Charlton W. *A History of Florida.* Rev. ed. Coral Gables: University of Miami, 1980.

Tolles, Bryant F., Jr. *The Grand Resort Hotels of the White Mountains.* Boston: David R. Godine, 1998.

Tuckwood, Jan, and Eliot Kleinberg. *Pioneers in Paradise: West Palm Beach, the First 100 Years*. Marietta, Ga.: Longstreet Press, 1994.

Veblen, Thorstein, *The Theory of the Leisure Class*. 1899. Reprint, New York: Penguin Books, 1994.

Villard, Henry S. *The Royal Victoria Hotel*. Nassau: Nassau Guardian, 1976.

Wagner, W. Sydney. "The Statler Idea in Hotel Planning and Equipment." *Architectural Forum*, November 1917.

_____. "The Statler Idea in Hotel Planning and Equipment." *Architectural Forum*, December 1917.

Weitze, Karen J. *California's Mission Revival*. Los Angeles: Hennessey and Ingalls, 1984.

White, Arthur. *Palaces of the People: A Social History of Commercial Hospitality*. London: Rapp and Whiting, 1968.

Williamson, Jefferson. *The American Hotel: An Anecdotal History*. New York: Knopf, 1930.

INDEX

Lightning Source UK Ltd.
Milton Keynes UK
UKHW012248231120
373929UK00002B/298